SHAREOLOGY

"There's nothing more misunderstood than the concept of 'influencers' and 'influencer marketing.' Kramer sets us straight on this, and gives us a MUCH better map towards a more meaningful success."
—**Chris Brogan**, CEO Owner Media Group

"Sharing isn't just a kindergarten fundamental. It's also a fundamental that the smartest businesses are embracing."
—**Ann Handley**, Chief Content Officer, MarketingProfs & Best Selling Author of *Everyone Writes*

"*Shareology* makes a compelling business case for the competitive advantage we can achieve by transparently and openly sharing knowledge, insights, methods, and especially our authentically quirky human-ness. The lessons can work on a personal level, as an individual professional, with an organization, and for entire businesses. Get the book! It puts wisdom into practice by sharing what you learn through the reactions and outcomes you experience."
—**Mark Yolton**, VP Digital Strategy & Enablement, Cisco

"Social sharing is the new currency of online business. Discover how to mine for social gold by digging into Bryan Kramer's book, *Shareology*."
—**Michael Stelzner**, Founder of Social Media Examiner and host of the Social Media Marketing podcast

"Bryan Kramer has done a stellar job of blending today's social technologies with the vital soft skills so needed for success in today's open and connected world. Technology has evolved radically in the last few years, but at the core, humans want to share and be acknowledged in order to belong, to connect, to know that we're important, that we matter. Entrepreneurs and mega brands alike are bound to see significant positive impact by studying Shareology and applying the teachings. Two thumbs way up!"

—**Mari Smith**, Author *The New Relationship Marketing*, Thought Leader & Premier Facebook Marketing Expert

"Sharing has always been an integral part of what we all do, but in the new world of social platforms and instantaneous output of content, understanding the hows and whys is essential. Bryan Kramer, in his inimitable fashion, lays it out for the reader... plain, simple, and easy to understand and implement."

—**Ted Rubin**, Author of *Return on Relationship*, Keynote Speaker, and Acting CMO of Brand Innovators

"In a heartfelt and investigative way, Bryan helps decode the sharing economy and build the justification for increased enterprise level sharing. Listening, sharing, and openness are difficult concepts for many companies to promote, yet consumers are increasingly demanding these attributes. Any organization that would like to develop impactful campaigns with different stakeholders to increase and justify sharing would benefit from Shareology."

—**Ari Lightman**, Professor, Digital Media and Marketing, The Heinz College, Carnegie Mellon University

"My mission is to connect big companies with customers using new technologies, so digital sharing is at the crux of what's important to me. Shareology teaches us why mastering the art and science of sharing is critical, and explains it in a way that's easy to understand, and actionable right now. For anyone else like me, who embraces sharing, Shareology is a must read."

—**Jeremiah Owyang**, Founder at Crowd Companies

"Brands, marketers, and anyone with a social media account are trying to find ways to connect with their audience. But the focus has been on manipulating content to make it more attractive. No one has taken us into the mind of consumers and what makes them want to share. It is not about building a better mousetrap, it is understanding what makes the mouse want the cheese."

—**Todd Wilms**, Head of Corporate Communications, Neustar

SHAREOLOGY

HOW SHARING IS POWERING
THE HUMAN ECONOMY

BRYAN KRAMER

New York

SHAREOLOGY
HOW SHARING IS POWERING THE HUMAN ECONOMY

© 2016 **BRYAN KRAMER**.

Published in New York, New York, by Morgan James Publishing. Morgan James and The Entrepreneurial Publisher are trademarks of Morgan James, LLC.
www.MorganJamesPublishing.com

The Morgan James Speakers Group can bring authors to your live event. For more information or to book an event visit The Morgan James Speakers Group at
www.TheMorganJamesSpeakersGroup.com.

A **free** eBook edition is available
with the purchase of this print book.

ISBN 978-1-63047-384-6 paperback
ISBN 978-1-63047-385-3 eBook
ISBN 978-1-63047-385-3 hardcover
Library of Congress Control Number:
2014946474

Cover Design by:
Rachel Lopez
www.r2cdesign.com

Interior Design by:
Bonnie Bushman
Caboodle Graphics

CLEARLY PRINT YOUR NAME ABOVE IN UPPER CASE
Instructions to claim your free eBook edition:
1. Download the BitLit app for Android or iOS
2. Write your name in **UPPER CASE** on the line
3. Use the BitLit app to submit a photo
4. Download your eBook to any device

In an effort to support local communities and raise awareness and funds, Morgan James Publishing donates a percentage of all book sales for the life of each book to Habitat for Humanity Peninsula and Greater Williamsburg.

Get involved today, visit
www.MorganJamesBuilds.com

Habitat for Humanity®
Peninsula and
Greater Williamsburg
Building Partner

DEDICATION

To Courtney, thank you for sharing your life with me.
To Emerson and Henry, never stop creating and smiling. Life is good.

TABLE OF CONTENTS

FREE ACCESS TO SHAREOLOGY PLATFORM

Claim your free membership to the Shareology Community Platform including bonuses and an opportunity to have your content featured in the community for book buyers only!

Bryan Kramer and the Shareology team would like to present you access to a number of free bonuses which are yours for the taking. As a book buyer, you are eligible to receive free reports, audio, video, and membership to the expertise from the following Shareology partners such as:

IBM, Neustar, MasterCard, Cisco, Hootsuite, Freshdesk, Speakeasy, Influitive, Mutual Mind, LittleBird, VentureBeat, Monster Products, and Cox Communications

To claim your spot and learn about the Shareology methodology, join the community here:

www.ShareologyBook.com

"In the human economy, the most valuable workers will be hired hearts."
—**Dov Seidman**, *Harvard Business Review*

ACKNOWLEDGMENTS

Many hours of labor and love went into creating this book, and I would like to thank everyone who had a hand in helping me get there:

To my wife, Courtney, whose unfailing support, insight, edits, reads and re-reads, research and writing support got us through sleepless nights and long weekends—to my partner in everything!

To my children, Emerson and Henry, for giving me the space to write while encouraging me to get out of my own brain sometimes. You two are the joys of my life from whom I draw my creativity and humor in everything we do together.

My parents, Richard and Leslie Kramer, who have always encouraged my brother and I to be creative in whatever we did in life including the most important emotion, happiness. We all learn to share from the moment we are born, and I'm happy to have learned this trait with my brother and best friend Seth Kramer.

To my posse, my dear friends, I can't thank you enough for helping me create through your awesomeness and support whether through discussions of sarcasm or moments of sincerity—a million thanks.

I also want to thank some of the behind-the scenes people who have helped me along the way: to my editor and friend, Apryl Parcher, thank you for your wordsmithing and valuable suggestions on how to bring out my voice; Maya Smith, who designed a great site and logo, and to David Hancock and the team at Morgan James publishing for being so easy to work with on this project.

To the entire PureMatter team, it takes a village and I can't thank you enough for the great brainstorming, ideas, support, creativity, and most of all….putting up with me through all of this.

In just the past five years, I've developed many social media friends. In fact, the power of social networking has expanded our horizons well beyond anything we could have imagined! Across the country and around the globe, these connections have helped me grow, and have made me some very dear friends. Through all the hangouts, tweet chats, interviews, conferences, tweets, posts, and likes, I'm grateful for our continued friendship.

To the expert contributors and business owners who added so much value to the pages of this book, I offer my eternal gratitude. Your stories and insights have added immeasurably to this effort, and I truly appreciate your willingness to share your time and expertise.

And finally, to our family dog, "fat Jessie". What can I say, thanks for keeping me company while I write and edit even in this moment as I type out the acknowledgements.

PART I
THE SHAREOLOGY
BACKSTORY

Sharing is a fundamental human behavior central to our survival as a human race. Whether we're sharing stories, processes, insights, philosophies, techniques, or secrets, it's how we connect to each other and advance as a society.

Now with technologies like the Internet, video, social media, and mobile, sharing has increased its ease and scale to a global level. Information is no longer confined to geographical boundaries; proximity is no longer required to pass information from one human to another.

This radical shift requires an understanding of how these technologies have impacted, and will continue to impact, our global society. Without this understanding of sharing patterns and analyzing what will resonate with other humans, ideas will be lost and change will be stifled.

How, what, why, and where we share as individuals in our new connected technological world has the power to influence and to effect change worldwide. After thirty thousand years of sharing information in the same way, yet faced in the last twenty years with the emergence of technologies that connect global tribes together, humans need to rethink the way we share ideas as a global community.

Now yes, this is all important to our communities, countries, and world. But the truth is, on a much more personal level, sharing saved my career.

After ten years as president of a Silicon Valley marketing firm, I was lost. I couldn't understand why; our multimillion-dollar business was thriving, showered with awards and global press. The operations, finance, and business development divisions were well-oiled machines. I found myself without a place to contribute to my own company. People were excited and eager to be a part of our business—everyone but me.

I contemplated quitting. I didn't have a purpose.

Desperate to connect to something, I found an unexpected kinship with social media. I don't care much for crowds or large groups of people; in fact, I am an introvert by nature, regaining my energy by being alone or with a trusted few. But over time I realized that social media gave me vast platforms to share my voice, my ideas, my contributions to anything and anyone—and people listened. They engaged, and I found myself wanting to figure out why. For three years I deconstructed these platforms and tried to understand why some ideas took off like wildfire and others died on the vine. I started to recognize patterns in sentiment and the importance of timing in making an idea explode into reality; and I connected and became social friends with some of the most inspirational thinkers in the world.

This experience profoundly affected my life, and it's what I chose to talk about when IBM asked me to speak at their TED (Technology, Entertainment and Design) event. More about that later.

Following the twists and turns of social philosophy and technology has made me an authentic leader and ushered me into what I believe is my destiny: to share what I've learned with others and change the way we think about communicating with one another.

So let's dive right into *Shareology*.

CHAPTER 1

THE IMPORTANCE
OF SHARING

Humans have been sharing resources and knowledge since they first banded together in prehistoric times, even before there was language. We shared to survive then, but we continue to share knowledge even though survival is no longer at stake. Or is it?

Philosophers have long pondered the nature of mankind and why we interact the way we do. We share for many reasons—some self-serving and some not—but I firmly believe that our need to share is based on the human instinct not only to survive, but to thrive.

Things are moving at a faster pace today for humankind than ever before, and we're more connected now than we've ever been. We're no longer polarized by geography, by race, by gender—but we still need each other to survive. Time has spread us across the globe, and the need to connect is written into our DNA, even though we're competing for the same limited space on this planet.

So what does this have to do with where we are today? Why is this important?

Because we're on the cusp of something big: a shift in human evolution.

Digital and Social Technologies Are Making a HUGE Impact

The Digital Age is a big part of this new shift in human evolution. The technology explosion of the last few years is teaching us to interact in a new way.

Social media, while it has had a big impact by itself, is just a piece of a bigger picture that is growing and expanding by the minute. It's exciting, but it's also a little scary. We're on the upward curve of a wave that's going to change our lives forever.

The digital and social technologies that have sprung up are connecting us to the rest of the world. That's the first part of this wave. The cusp I referred to earlier—the top of the wave—is that these technologies and ways of communicating are also transforming our physical world.

For example, 3-D printers, the stuff of science fiction just a decade or two ago, are now allowing us to manufacture parts and materials— from biomaterials and implants for the medical industry to aerospace technologies and manufacturing—that transform the way we live. We can even print clothing and food. Imagine the impact this will have when 3-D printing technology becomes commonplace (and it's getting there). We'll be able to order things like jackets, gourmet meals, or cars and have them printed and delivered immediately—or even print them ourselves in the comfort of our own home.

Another example is the sensors that connect things and people, such as wearable technology like Apple Watch and Fitbit. Even the Tesla self-driving car that can navigate and steer its way to any destination demonstrates the rapid evolution of technologies that connect our digital and physical world. At this point, we are limited only by our imaginations regarding what could be next.

Resisting the Cocoon

In our lifetimes we've seen some pretty amazing things come to pass. Back in 1991, I read a book that I'll never forget—*The Popcorn Report*[1] by Faith Popcorn. It outlined her predictions about the impact of technologies that enable us to cocoon in our homes. The idea was that we'd no longer need to coexist outside. Everything would be delivered. You could work from home because everything would be remote. People would have Internet connections, remote conferences, watch keynotes on big screens without leaving their bedrooms. Anything you would need to eat, sleep, and work would all be deliverable within your own space. Well, that's all here now. Just a little over twenty years later, we are technologically enabled to safely cocoon in our homes without sacrificing anything we need to survive.

Amazon, Google Express, and Instacart are prime examples of brands that are making this concept real for us today. Their next-day and same-day delivery of goods and services fills a need that we have been clamoring for: saving time. Frankly, I've tried to beat their system, ordering just one small item like a container of dental floss or placing a huge order then choosing a delivery time to my house just a few hours later. In every instance, they come through with delivery as promised, with a smile. How do they do that?

The Digital Age has made everyone busier, more accessible, and managing more devices, so saving time is a big deal. However, what's happened in the last decade has profoundly affected us socially. Most all of us have experienced a decrease in our connection with each other physically because we can "connect" online. The things Faith Popcorn predicted weren't science fiction. They were just the beginning

1   Popcorn, Faith. *The Popcorn Report.* New York: HarperCollins, 1991.

of this big new shift. But there's more coming, and it's important to understand what that will look like, and the way it will impact us as people and as brands.

As humans, the thought of totally cocooning creeps us out a bit. We don't want to think that we will exist just in our homes and never venture outside. With reality TV shows like *Hoarders* or movies that depict people who struggle with agoraphobia (the fear of being outside), Hollywood makes us cringe at the idea. Although technology makes it easier to insulate ourselves, we still need to leave the house, or at the very least, step outside our front doors.

Why? Because our biggest need as humans is connection. I'm not talking about basic needs like food, shelter, and clothing. I'm talking about the need to find a tribe. Our need to belong. Our need to contribute to something greater than ourselves and be acknowledged for it by another human. Social ceases to exist without it, because people must connect with other people. We crave it. We'll fight for it. Who wants a world without family reunions, anniversaries, and dinner with friends?

So Why Do We Share at All?
In my research for this book I interviewed more than one hundred people to figure out what motivates us to share. What I've discovered is that behind all the reasons people say we share, whether it's to help someone, make them laugh, or alert them to something, there is really only one reason at the core of human sharing: self-perception.

Now, before you start ranting, "But wait, Bryan, that seems too selfish a reason; there has to be something deeper," let me explain.

Our own estimation of ourselves means a lot to each one of us because that's our identity as humans. We also care about what others think of us because we need to connect with them and belong to a tribe, and to do this we need to align ourselves with other humans. In the marketing world, this is branding. And as humans, because technology has empowered us to share with our global tribe, it's never been more important to treat ourselves as a *personal brand*.

Creating and sharing information is important, but creating and sharing our personal brand is what shapes the way people perceive us and connects us to the tribes that matter.

To help put a little science around this, my team and I spent quite a bit of time pondering the legitimacy of this formula:

© 2015 Bryan Kramer

This formula shows that personal reputation is equal to the perceived reputation of the content or source that's being shared. In other words, I will only share something with others that is in line with how I perceive myself and how I want to be perceived. Do I identify with being "the first to know"? If I did, I would probably share content I felt was late-breaking news. Do I identify with being humorous? Then I would share jokes or other things I thought were funny. Do I want others to see me as a helpful connector? Then I would probably share information directly with someone I thought I could help.

Most of this is done unconsciously because we're all very multidimensional, non-self-actualized, busy humans.

However, when you consciously recognize your own personal brand, whether it be creativity, love, justice, humor, science, or whatever you truly love and care about, then the ideas you share will connect you to others that care about the same thing.

But what about brands that are trying to build online communities and build relationships? How can they thrive in a digital world?

The Secret Sauce for Brands

As far as brands are concerned, one of the biggest shortcomings of the Digital Age is the disconnection between their own self-recognition as an entity and the individual humans they're trying to serve. Brands most often turn to technology first to make quick connections at scale but forget what makes people want to interact with them in the first place—a human-to-human connection. This is especially true on social channels.

We've all heard the axiom that our customers are at the center of our business, and that our brand reputations are now in the hands of the consumer. That may be true, but how can these brands compete in a social space where the scales have tipped and consumers have more control?

As my friend Jay Baer says about social platforms, "You're not just competing with other brands for their attention, you're also competing with their friends, family, music playlists, soccer games, and nights out on the town."

It's a noisy feed out there, each one being different, unique, and personalized to each individual user. The one thing you have in your favor? When you understand why we share and how we interact with each other, you regain a place as a potential friend to your customers instead of being perceived by them as a cold, insensitive entity with no redeeming aspects with which to connect. If this isn't a competitive advantage, I don't know what is.

We want our social followers to share what we have to say, and we become disappointed when they don't. But are you saying anything that's worthy of sharing? Does what you share fill a human need or desire? Have you connected with people in a way that strikes a chord? What is it that makes a piece of social communication shareable?

The Shareability Quotient

To help brands share, we developed what we call "The Shareability Quotient."

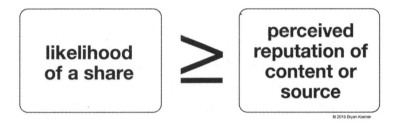

Much like a personal brand, no doubt your company has built a brand around a set of core values that reflect what's important to your audience. They perceive your brand as either a trusted source or as having insightful, helpful, funny, or valuable content. The Shareability Quotient says that the likelihood of a share is greater than or equal to the perceived reputation of your content or trust as a source.

In other words, if you want people to share your stuff, they need to trust you or identify with the content you're producing, period.

For them to trust your brand, you need to:

- Work on humanizing every single interaction (embrace your imperfections).
- Know what they care about (empathize).
- Know what you stand for as a brand (simplify).
- Do the hard work to create content that is shareable (communicate).

In other words, being human means being shareable.

Brands must embody sharing as a guiding principle far beyond the social realm. They need to acknowledge its importance not just in messaging but also in their human interaction across their entire company experience. Knowing how your business mindfully chooses to share with your customers and prospects, how it interplays in the interaction with your peers, your employees—even your competitors— can make the difference between success and failure.

To survive this evolutionary shift that's coming, we all need to find ways to embrace the social and digital wave that's cresting right now— use its momentum and align ourselves to influence human experience. It's time to define our sharing principles.

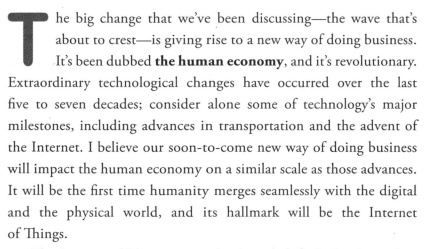

CHAPTER 2

SHARING IN THE
HUMAN ECONOMY

T he big change that we've been discussing—the wave that's about to crest—is giving rise to a new way of doing business. It's been dubbed **the human economy**, and it's revolutionary. Extraordinary technological changes have occurred over the last five to seven decades; consider alone some of technology's major milestones, including advances in transportation and the advent of the Internet. I believe our soon-to-come new way of doing business will impact the human economy on a similar scale as those advances. It will be the first time humanity merges seamlessly with the digital and the physical world, and its hallmark will be the Internet of Things.

The Internet of Things is a technological shift that's taking place right now where physical devices are being digitally connected to create more value. According to Gartner Inc., there will be nearly 26 billion devices on the Internet of Things by 2020.[2] Technology giants like IBM and Cisco have been working on this for several years. In fact, Cisco even goes so far as to call this evolution the "Internet of Everything." I spoke to Blair Christie, chief marketing officer of Cisco, about this in one of my company PureMatter's *Substance* interviews. She talked about the concept, in the context of value, and how it changes the face of business and our lives as a whole:

> The Internet of Everything is basically the next wave. It's how people, process, data, and things are connecting in a way that hasn't happened before. For instance, we think we're connected today, but less than 1 percent of the world is actually connected to the Internet. Today that's less than 2 billion people. By 2020 it will be close to 5 billion. Right now 20 to 25 billion things are connected to the Internet— by 2020 close to 50 billion things will be connected. That's remarkable! We're already having machine-to-machine or thing-to-thing doing a lot of interacting, but we will be seeing more people-to-machine, machine-to-people, and people-to-people connecting and providing more value in that connection than we've ever seen before.

Blair Christie believes that moving beyond the Internet of Things to fully embrace the Internet of Everything is where the real value lies for people, and I agree. When everything at home and everything at work is connected, it will fundamentally change our lives.

Today, sharing communities are making it easier for individuals to get goods and services from each other (not just from brands), and this has produced new disruptive business models. Whether it's

---

2   Middleton, P., Kjeldsen, P., & Tully, J. (2013) *Forecast: The Internet of Things, Worldwide*. Retrieved from Gartner database.

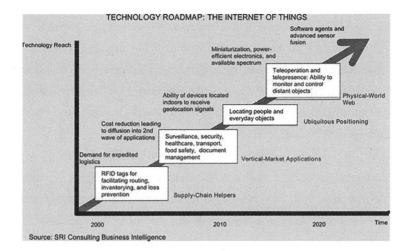

sharing or buying pre-owned or custom products (eBay, Craigslist, Pleygo, Etsy), providing services (Elance, ODesk, Angie's List), or transportation (Car2Go, Uber, or Zipcar), people are moving toward a more collaborative mode of doing business with each other, and that's forcing industries to change the way they approach relationships with consumers.

In November 2014, I attended the **3DEXPERIENCE FORUM**, a conference held by Dassault Systemes in Las Vegas. I was fascinated by the magic behind how virtual reality could help plan and build toward greater human experiences. Quite frankly, I thought I was attending a conference about technology. I was wrong, very wrong.

Several keynotes stuck out, including one from Honda. Company representatives explained how testing in virtual systems allows for an understanding of every possible car crash scenario, which provides a true perspective of how to build safe and well-designed cars with the right parts. The forum also featured a virtual recreation of a beating heart (which looked so real you couldn't tell the difference). With the aid of 3-D glasses, the demonstration showed spinning, dissecting, and new ways for doctors to perform surgery before they ever operate. This technology is a direct result of customers' demands for companies to deliver something extraordinarily different. "Loyalty and its definition has changed overnight," said Ken Clayton, vice president of Dassault Systemes. "Customers have gone in a direction for reasons we didn't understand. And now the experience has to speak through our products. Customers expect and deserve a personal experience."

During the demonstration, a discussion on collaboration on top of computation provided a real *aha* moment for me. Imagine a group of people meeting via video to build three-dimensional products virtually and to overlay their independent work to look for inconsistencies together. Witnessing thousands of computations involving a deep level of math in real time in a truly collaborative experience blew me away.

Collaboration will play a big role in building the experiences of the future. "A complete software experience must include HR plus sales plus marketing plus 3-D applications in order to be successful," said Monica Menghini, executive vice president of Dassault. "Each touchpoint has an engaged process that can make or break the end result or customer experience." Dassault made it clear to me that we can now do this through a collaborative social process using their virtual technology.

Business heads like Jeremiah Owyang, founder of Crowd Companies, are leaders in the Collaborative Economy movement, which is all about the convergence of the physical and digital worlds. In fact, a report called "Sharing Is the New Buying,"[3] cocreated by Crowd Companies and the community technology company Vision Critical, surveyed over ninety thousand customers across the US, Canada, and the UK to see how they are participating in today's collaborative business environment. The results are an astonishing indicator of how powerful sharing is right now and how much more powerful it will be in the years to come.

---

3   Owyang, J., Samuel, A., Grenville, A. "Sharing Is the New Buying." http://tms.visioncritical.com/sites/default/files/pdf/sharing-new-buying-collaborative-economy-report.pdf. (accessed February 20, 2015).

Owyang captured his vision of the collaborative business movement in a "Honeycomb" graphic, a visual representation that's "organized info families, classes and startup examples." The first version illustrated six industries, but just seven months later, the second version (released December 7, 2014) had twelve (view it here: http://www.web-strategist. com/blog/2014/12/07/collaborative-economy-honeycomb-2-watch-it-grow/).

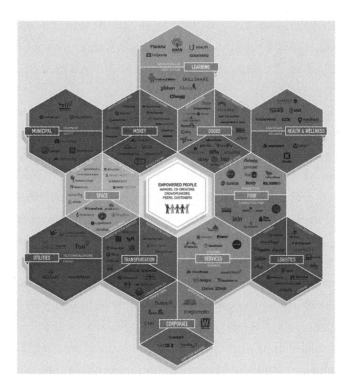

One of my favorite examples of a collaborative business is the disruptive transportation company Uber, which allows an individual to easily schedule a ride online, in real time, sourced from a team of Uber drivers in the area. This is something taxis historically could never do (they're scrambling to catch up but not without global controversy that has sometimes turned violent). The power of the crowd makes it work because after your ride, you rate your driver with one to five stars, and they in turn rate you. Good drivers work hard to get excellent ratings, which is what makes this model work.

I know this firsthand—I use the service regularly for rides to and from the airport. In a recent trip to LA, my Uber driver had loaded up his iPad with Spotify tunes so we could jam to our favorite music all the way back to our hotel—he got a five-star rating from me! In Dallas once, a driver accidentally took me to the wrong terminal and had already shut off the app and charged me. Rather than let me walk, he drove me to the right terminal for no additional charge. Another five stars!

Aside from the price and convenience, the Uber experience itself is another reason they're so popular. When the driver picks you up, he or she knows your name and comes around just like any quality driver would, greets you, and puts your bags in the back. Usually, fresh bottles of water are waiting for you. The digital app has given them all the information they need about you to personalize your experience. The company's lower cost UberX service, on the other hand, is a bit more of a crapshoot. UberX allows riders to be picked up in the driver's personal car, so you don't always know what you're going to get. One UberX driver picked us up in a beat-up car and threw our luggage in his trunk full of trash. He did not get a five-star rating to say the least.

You might think that quality control would be a problem with drivers who are essentially free agents, but drivers have gone out of their way to help me on several occasions, and not a single one has been rude. As of this writing, Uber has gotten into some hot water, with accusations of violence toward a rider, and the CEO has been criticized for misogynistic business practices. I sincerely hope both are not true, because both would cause me to think twice about using them again.

Until I hear otherwise, I will still use Uber (unless they're in surge pricing mode) because I know the experience is going to be consistent—much more consistent than taxis.

Google Express is another great example. It's an online service that hand delivers goods within hours of your order. The delivery person drives a Google-Express-branded car and arrives wearing a Google Express T-shirt and bearing goods from local partner stores like Target, Walgreens, Costco, REI, Whole Foods, Office Depot, and Staples. It's the best of both worlds: locally sourced goods help support my community, and I don't have to leave my couch to get them. Remember Faith Popcorn's "cocooning"? I'm living it. Right now it's a free trial service only available in select cities, but I'm hoping it catches on everywhere.

My family's first experience with Google Express happened when our toaster broke on a Saturday morning. Knowing we'd want toast on Sunday, we used the Google Express app to place an order for a toaster (which happened to come from Target) as well as some other things we needed—and *voilà*! Within six hours, Tony, our Google Express guy, showed up with everything at our door, neatly bagged and sealed. We found the experience to be super convenient and fun.

The tagline on their packaging says it all: *Contains one less errand to run.* Perfect. The next time we used the service, our dog, Jessie, started barking when the delivery guy opened our front gate. My daughter scooped Jessie up to calm her down and said, "Don't worry, Jessie! It's just Google at the door."

Wait. Google at the door? It may have been known as an online search company, but today Google is a "results delivered" company, ready to please its customers virtually or in physical form. Think about how Google started and how much they've changed their paradigm thanks to technology, sharing, and cultural mindset. Pretty mind-blowing if you ask me.

Another good example of a business that owes its success to the collaborative economy is Airbnb, the shared space broker that's shaking up the hospitality industry. They've combined the power of sourcing the crowd with a social e-commerce engine. It connects people who need lodging to people who want to offer their home, condo, or apartment when they're not using it. For travelers, Airbnb offers rates that are generally cheaper than hotels and a great customer experience. For property owners, the platform provides the opportunity to make money renting out what they own (during short, specific dates) and a readymade audience who want this service.

The new sharing model puts power into the hands of homeowners and traveling consumers and is changing the way many people book overnight stays. For instance, the renowned film, music, and digital festival South by Southwest (SXSW) that happens each March in Austin, Texas, has grown exponentially due to Airbnb. Prior to Airbnb, attendance was limited by hotel availability. Now more attendees descend on Austin during the few weeks of the event, providing Austin-area property owners (and I'm sure renters and leasers) opportunities to make money leasing their spaces at a premium. I can attest to this personally. My wife and I were customers of Airbnb during SXSW and would have been stuck in a two-star hotel in the boonies if it weren't for an awesome studio condo we found within walking distance to downtown. I feel good about it too. We've gotten to know the owner, and the money we pay for the week is helping her put a serious dent in grad school. Airbnb for the win!

Some even use Airbnb as a business. In a *Fast Company* article called "Secrets of Running a Six-Figure Airbnb Business,"[4] author Sarah Kessler describes an options trader in San Francisco who makes trades until the early afternoon, then spends the rest of the day managing six apartments he rents to Airbnb guests, netting about $2,000 profit per apartment per month after expenses. Airbnb charges a modest fee for their service but even so is making quite a profit as well. At this writing, Airbnb has pushed the company's valuation to $10 billion, making it more valuable than long-established hotel chains around the world such as Wyndham, Hyatt, and InterContinental—*all without owning a single piece of property.*

Taking It to the Next Level

So as the human economy matures, how can Airbnb further improve the experience it offers? After all, long-established companies like Hilton and Hyatt have earned more trust from consumers as known brands. Unless you've tried Airbnb, you have no experience with it—and trust is built over time.

The answer? New collaborations. Imagine if Hilton started a property accreditation program and cobranded with property owners to create "Hilton Endorsed" Airbnb rentals. After a thorough review by Hilton to get its stamp of approval, the rental could use Hilton linens, toiletries—even maid service. If you saw the Hilton logo on an Airbnb property, wouldn't you trust it more? Of course you would! Combine that big-brand credibility with the surprise of a wonderful experience, and you've really got something—a win-win powered by the human economy.

And how about Uber? Imagine how the integration of your social behavior and personal data could make our physical world experiences

---

4   http://www.fastcompany.com/3021179/secrets-of-running-a-six-figure-airbnb-business

even more highly unique and shareable. For instance, what if the data Uber collects about you in their app (location, destination, in-car experiences, water brand preference, etc.) could be integrated with third-party information like your airline rewards program or shopping preferences? What if this information could be transferred to the hotel's check-in system in the instant they dropped you off at the entrance? As you walked into the hotel, this information would pop up onscreen and you'd be greeted by name by the front desk clerk, who also digitally awards you frequent flyer points and orders your favorite water up to your room in seconds—all without you changing your behavior in the physical world (#mindblown). It's all headed here, and community is at the core of this impending change. As the human economy grows, we're going to see more of this kind of innovation.

This is all new ground, and radical changes are ahead for society as a whole as we learn to blend more digital technology into our physical world. As the human economy unfolds, we need to be cautious and understand what we're agreeing to undertake. It won't happen overnight. Society will warm up to these new technologies in stages, which is the way we've always adjusted to new things. You can't change someone's background or how they grew up or easily change thinking patterns that have become ingrained. Some will adopt it readily while others will resist. For instance, 2012 Pew Research on older adults and technology usage[5] indicates that for the first time, more than half of older adults (59 percent of those surveyed aged sixty-five or older) report to be Internet users, with 47 percent indicating their homes are equipped with a high-speed broadband connection. A large majority of older adults have also adopted cell phones. Yet these high rates of adoption are limited to

5   Smith, Aaron, "Older Adults and Technology Use," *Pew Research Center,*
      published April 2, 2014, accessed February 4, 2015, http://www.pewinternet.
      org/2014/04/03/older-adults-and-technology-use/

younger, higher-income, or more highly educated seniors, and only 18 percent of them own a smartphone. About a quarter use social networks like Facebook.

In contrast, another Pew study on Millennials[6] (eighteen to thirty-three-year-olds) shows that not only are they digital natives, they're the most avid users of these technologies—especially social platforms. The vast majority (81 percent) are on Facebook and have larger friend counts than older age groups.

When will we get there? We're probably a generation away. The tipping point will be when Millennials are fully in place in our workforce and become the new thirty- and forty-somethings. The human economy's growth will be stagnated by "business as usual" until consumers (en masse) force brands to innovate outside their comfort zones.

Integrating Social

Another crucial piece of sharing in the human economy is social media. Let's say I've just had a great experience with Uber or Airbnb or Google Express. There should be a means available that allows me to immediately share my experience without me having to log in on the computer or open an app. Catching people in the moment is crucial. Businesses understand how important it is for people to share their experiences, but they haven't yet embedded social sharing into the experience in real time—and they need to wake up.

I'm a very social person, so I made time to take that picture of my Google Express experience and post it on Twitter and Facebook. But what if I could do that directly from the app, the car, or from home at the very moment I'm being delighted? Making it super-easy to share on any channel in real time is another vital piece of what's coming in the

6 "Millennials in Adulthood," *Pew Research Center*, published March 7, 2014, accessed February 4, 2015, http://www.pewsocialtrends.org/2014/03/07/millennials-in-adulthood/

human economy. The social experience is becoming increasingly blended into our lives, and brands will have to learn to integrate that too.

That's where I see the shareable experiences heading: you'll start to see these kinds of things integrate into our lives because brands will have to partner with people to offer a unique, delightful experience that's personally tailored to the user. They'll also be coming up with new, innovative ways to socially share that experience in real time.

CHAPTER 3

THE IMPORTANCE
OF CONTEXT

What Is Context?

I n the new human economy, understanding context is crucial to achieving success in business. Before the advent of social media, companies relied on focus groups to gather contextual information about people's interactions with products. This information helped them design products that fit into the lives of their target market. In the late '90s a system called context mapping was used to gather this type of information to aid in the design process.[7] However, assembling the focus group, gathering data, and building a context map for designers was a time-consuming, cumbersome path to innovation. Traditional focus groups are dead.

---

7   *CoDesign: International Journal of CoCreation in Design and the Arts,* Vol. 1 No. 2: "Contextmapping: experiences from practice" Taylor and Francis, 2005

In today's hyperconnected world, the focus group is everywhere online, and brands are in a mad scramble to gather usable information quickly—and not just from one small focus group, but from millions of people across the globe. To innovate faster, you're in a race against time to get as much information as you can about your prospects. New technologies allow us to do that by listening to the conversations already taking place across the Web and by delving into social conversation with individuals to crowdsource the design process.

An array of focus groups exists in a multitude of places online—Facebook, Twitter, LinkedIn, blogs—and more are coming online each day, each with its own language and way of doing things. Even the cover of this book was crowdsourced to find a favorite image. I posted three choices on Facebook and got over two hundred comments and opinions about which one was the frontrunner. As a "brand" myself, I care more about what real potential consumers of my book think than a group of randoms locked in a room behind a glass wall.

Understanding context means understanding all factors that influence an experience, which also includes how people talk about it (and with whom). Where are people talking? What are the rules of conversation? Why are they using a particular platform or technology? Because there are so many different ways to have conversations today, it's more important than ever to understand not just the context of a person's experience with your product or service, but also the various ways they could share that experience and how we can facilitate that sharing.

You always have to be mindful of context when you share, and in my earlier book, *Human to Human: #H2H*, I listed four ways I try to do that before deploying any social effort, which is valuable to repeat here:

The Four Rules of Social Context

1. **Think it through:** (or, as Courtney Smith, our company cofounder and executive creative director, likes to say, TITS: Think It Through SERIOUSLY). To do this, whether it's a blog or a tweet, you need to visualize how what you share will play out and whether it meets your objectives. Everything you share should be true to your brand (personal and company) to support your goals and have a purpose. When it isn't, you may be digging your own grave. Almost weekly, I hear of someone getting fired for mistakenly tweeting something inappropriate, either from their own handle or a corporate handle. This can be avoided by simply thinking it through (seriously.)

2. **Skip to the last page first:** In other words, know the end as well as the beginning when you plan your strategy. This is the difference between creating something complicated versus complex. Complex systems work because there's a beginning and an end point, with the trick being figuring out the best way to connect the two points. Complicated systems have one or the other. You don't want to lead your audience down a path that just starts meandering—they'll likely not stick with you. You have to know what direction you're heading in with your message. Always. P.S. Don't deviate. And if you do, redefine the end.

3. **Slow down:** How many times have you tweeted, posted, blogged, updated—just pushed a message out there so you can check it off your list? We live in a fast-paced world where if you move too quickly, you forget to put effort into the moment that could potentially be a creative and thoughtful experience. Courtney always says that when she gets behind a computer, time slows down and she enters a time warp. I don't know how she does it, but she always comes out with the most incredible creative

product and has learned to harness time and not rush the process. When you take time to reflect on what you're creating, you'll enter your audience's world—and then you'll deliver a message that will resonate.

4. **Get out of your head:** It's time to break out of that old habit of thinking everyone knows what's rattling around in your brain. Look at what you're sharing from an outsider's point of view. Before you post something, ask someone on your staff, a friend, or a colleague if it makes sense to them. Get objective opinions. Be *you*, yes—be true to your thoughts and opinions, but express them in a way that people will understand you. Sometimes that means sharing your own context along with your message.

Contextual Shape-Shifting

As technology continues to evolve, especially in the digital space, we find ourselves shape-shifting from the digital world into the physical and vice versa, moving conversation, collaboration, and sharing from one context to another.

Let's take the physical realm of shape-shifting and look at the latest MIT project, a display that enables you to reach through a screen and affect an object on the other side. Imagine being on Skype with your friends and the camera picks up the movement of your hands. The movement allows you to physically move the object in front of the computer on the other end. While the immediate applications are small, the potential impact is endless in high sensory experiences such as medical procedures, cooking lessons in your own kitchen, and high-touch education.

Shape-shifting also applies to the contextual moments we rely on to gather information. You would be surprised to think of Apple's

Siri as a limited database, but it is; this is why it doesn't always pull the information you need based on what you ask of the technology. However, in Apple's latest patent application, Siri will be able to reach beyond its available data and take the cumulative thoughts from human interactions across digital and social, and crowdsource the information just for you.

Shared and connected experiences will give rise to many more innovations like these that will help us cross-contextualize lines in communication and sharing. We're at the very beginning and cannot even imagine how our lives will change over the next five to ten years. However, one essential thing will never change: the human need to communicate with each other as individuals. Recently I met Faith Popcorn for the first time and heard firsthand her predictions for what our lives will look like in 2050. As excited as I was to hear her perspective (after all, her first book, *The Popcorn Report*, greatly influenced my own career), I was not excited by what I learned.

According to Faith, the future looks, well ... *grim*. It's dystopian, with a fourth robot class displacing human workers and humans essentially living in isolated pods, only communicating via technology. In her vision, everything we need, including food, is served to us in our own personal environment. There's no reason to leave our homes, no physical reason to connect, no need unfillable. As someone who stands for human-to-human connection, this was hard for me to wrap my head around. Don't we have a choice? Will we choose, as human beings, to blindly evolve into a society that prioritizes things and efficiency over emotion? I hope not. Technology may be driving new ways to connect and converse, but we should keep in mind that human conversation drives business. And soon technology will allow us to deliver *personalized* and *individualized* experiences between humans and brand marketers, delivering real-time opportunities to speak human to human, as it should be.

Personalizing the Experience

Businesses have been using personalization in marketing for a long time, from addressing prospects by name in direct mail to delivering different versions of digital content that's tailored to specific audiences. However, as technology moves us forward and audiences become more selective about the information they choose to absorb, it becomes more important to use a holistic approach to personalization—collecting and using the kind of data that can personalize an individual's entire experience with your brand.

Rob Gatto, senior vice president of sales at Neustar, a data intelligence company, defines personalization as "providing someone in a communication a special version that is predicated for them." There are personalization opportunities in digital channels such as websites, search, newsfeeds, and social media, and there are also personalization options in offline environments like call centers. In all of these channels, given the right type of intelligence, companies can tailor the experience to individuals based on what they know about the person or the person's past actions.

Rob uses theme parks as a good example of how personalization can be used to enhance a person's experience via a call center:

> So, let's say I'm an employee in a theme park call center. And let's say a husband (or maybe a wife) has set up a spring break trip for my theme park online, and one of them calls in with a question. When I answer the phone, I make the connection between the husband, wife, or household's existing reservation. I reach into the CRM database, pull it up, and now I'm able to answer, "Well, hi, Mr. Gatto. I'm glad to hear from you! I see that you're coming to the theme park three weeks from today; what can I help you with?" During the course of the conversation, I might see an opportunity such as, "I see you don't have any theme park dinners with Mickey

or Minnie," or whatever theme park it may happen to be. "May I suggest a character breakfast or a character dinner?"

Rob is particularly excited about the future of personalization because there are now more opportunities for brands to individually tailor messages and advertise them to individuals on various channels.

What is really cool is linking all those channels together for one view of the customer, and then coordinating your messaging across those channels. Whether it's a website, call center, display ad, search campaign, or social, understanding how all those things interact with one another in the customer's life gives me the power to sequence the messaging so it makes sense to that person; it's coordinated, and it's going into the right channels. The company's advantage is extinguishing waste—not advertising in different channels with different messages, but having a coordinated effort, or maybe not advertising at all in some channels.

I also think there's an opportunity for knowing how I (as a potential customer) might react in the digital world differently than my daughter or my son or my wife. For instance, you might not get me on my phone or my iPad, but you might get me on my laptop. You may never reach my wife on her laptop; you may only get her on her iPad. So there are opportunities not only for personalizing a message, but also for understanding how people like to be communicated with and which channels are likely to get the best response rate.

We also talked about how this level of personalization can affect a brand's shareability. When data is used correctly to enhance experience, trust goes up, which factors into the Shareability Quotient discussed earlier. "It's learning from the customers you have, so that when you're pursuing new customers, you have a better idea of what experience to deliver to them based on likeminded profiles," Rob says. "The more information that customers share about themselves at any point of interaction, the more personalized we can make their experience at other connection points—the bank teller, checkout, or 800 number. One of the interesting things to consider for the future is how to tie those channels together so that your interaction with an individual is consistent across all of them."

Rob's absolutely right. The better we get to know our customers as individuals, the better we'll become at delivering the personalized attention people want from our brands. Technology gives us the tools to gather more data and communicate across more channels, but it's up to us to use those tools to provide value, build trust, and conduct business with a human touch.

CHAPTER 4

THE HUMAN
BUSINESS MOVEMENT

Human to Human

W hen my first book *Human to Human: #H2H* came out, I received thousands of comments and shares because people truly desire a more human approach to marketing, to human resources, to customer service, to sales—just about everything that has to do with business. Over the last year, the concept has continued to resonate and grow as a key business tenet. More and more people are embracing the concept of human business, and it's awesome. In fact, in January 2015, The Writer, a language consultancy, conducted a scientific study with its readers and they voted "H2H" (Human to Human) as the number one business buzzword most likely to dominate the coming year![8]

---

8   http://www.prnewsonline.com/water-cooler/2014/12/26/infographic-what-business-words-will-take-off-in-2015/#.VKa20saxrL5.twitter

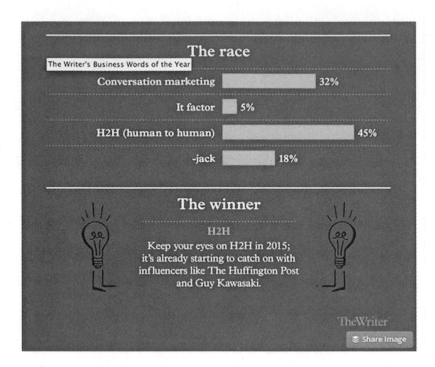

Every company and person should operate from an H2H foundation. After all, everything has to be done in collaboration with somebody to make something work. Whether it's developing products, coming up with a business solution, or communicating in general, H2H is the foundation. It's also the bridge between connecting the internal company and the external company.

Todd Wilms, vice president of digital at Neustar, remarked on how our corporate leadership is being pressed to be more human in his blog post "The Surprising Rise of the Human Executive"[9]:

---

9   Wilms, Todd, "The Surprising Rise of the Human Executive," *Bryan Kramer (blog)*, http://bryankramer.com/the-surprising-rise-of-the-human-executive/.

Over the last 10 years we have seen a dramatic rise in the more human side of our executives. This has not been caused by our leadership suddenly joining support groups, seeking counseling, or—as HBO's comedy *Silicon Valley* would have you believe— going on a drug fueled vision quest. Our executive class has become more human because the markets and the customers have demanded it.

I agree with Todd, but there are challenges that many people still struggle with. I talked to Kim Garst of Boom Social about this, and she agrees that being human online is a big challenge for many businesses.

From my experience I think that people struggle with this the most. For all of the businesses that we've worked with, bringing the human side to their brand has been a huge, huge struggle for them. It's something they have to learn. They have to get more comfortable in their own skin with it.

For example, one of the biggest questions that I get from people is, "What do I say on social media?" And my response is always, "Well, what would you say if you were standing in front of somebody?" They struggle with the concept of "it's a keyboard," and they're putting written words out there that they want to make sure are perfect. What do I say? How do I make sure I'm saying it right? Are people going to like what I say? There is a big laundry list of concerns that people have.

Kim went on to say that after a person stops hiding behind their logo and corporate image and chooses to be "real," people will finally connect with them. This phenomenon is not linked to business size— big or small, if you're "real" with your customers, the results will be the same. Let people see behind the curtain, and their engagement with your business will skyrocket. I've found this to be true in my own company. When I stepped out from behind PureMatter with my own social footprint, connections and opportunities really began to scale.

From an internal and external standpoint, humanization is a big differentiator in business. Just look at *Fortune*'s "Best Places to Work" list. What do you think are the criteria for being on that list? Being people-centric is near the top, as well as having a collaborative atmosphere. When companies value their employees' contributions and create a collaborative environment with open communication, great things happen. Repeatedly revealed in *Fortune*'s case studies are direct links between a more human workplace culture and remarkable business success. These are evidenced by gains in stock price, revenue, profitability, and other key financial indicators.

Companies such as Google and SAS top the *Fortune* list, but here's an example of the power of sharing from Zappos, as illustrated in an article from BioTalent Canada[10]: "When Chase Adams moved to Las Vegas to start a job at Zappos, he arrived with his wife and a truck full of belongings. Before he could unpack, his new team from Zappos showed up to help. Within a few hours, he felt at home and had made strong connections at Zappos. In Adams's words, it was 'the most ridiculously amazing welcome' to his new job."

This is good old-fashioned being neighborly, and when we translate that to our businesses, it's a win-win. This is true for employees, customers, vendors, and partners. The more human your interactions with everyone, the more relationships will blossom and the more success you'll enjoy. Giving value, sharing stories and information, being the

---

10   Ross, Pam. "Workplace Culture: Humanizing Your Organization," BioTalent Canada, http://www.biotalent.ca/en/article/workplace-culture-humanizing-your-organization.

go-to resource, helping people solve their problems—all of these human activities make us more attractive as brands to the people we want to employ and do business with.

Being a Leader in the Human Economy

It would seem that succeeding in the human economy may be easier on a peer-to-peer level. After all, being "neighborly" and collaborating and communicating in a way that builds mutual trust and respect seems to imply a "fair exchange of value." But how can business leaders also embrace a human approach to their leadership style without breaking a corporate structure, overstepping boundaries, or oversharing?

By definition, #H2H means bringing back the human side of communication in all its simplicity, empathy, and imperfection. In many ways, this is in direct alignment with *emotional intelligence*, an emerging new success measurement that assesses for the "X-factor," traits that make someone likeable, trusted, and more approachable—all the best parts of a human in business. According to an article by Daniel Goleman in *Harvard Business Review*,[11] emotional intelligence is a group of five components that enable the best leaders to maximize their own and their followers' performance. These components are:

- **Self-Awareness**: The ability to recognize and understand your moods, emotions, and drives, as well as their effect on others.
- **Self-Regulation:** The ability to control or redirect disruptive impulses and moods; the propensity to suspend judgment and think before acting.
- **Motivation:** A passion to work for reasons that go beyond money or status; a propensity to pursue goals with energy and persistence.

---

11   Goleman, Daniel, "What Makes a Leader," Emotional Intelligence, *Harvard Business Review*, January 2004, https://hbr.org/2004/01/what-makes-a-leader.

- **Empathy:** The ability to understand the emotional makeup of other people; skill in treating people according to their emotional reactions.
- **Social Skill:** Proficiency in managing relationships and building networks; an ability to find common ground and build rapport.

Each component, as the chart here shows, demonstrates "Hallmarks"—actions that show varying levels of emotional intelligence.

The Five Components of Emotional Intelligence at Work

	Definition	Hallmarks
Self-Awareness	the ability to recognize and understand your moods, emotions, and drives, as well as their effect on others	self-confidence realistic self-assessment self-deprecating sense of humor
Self-Regulation	the ability to control or redirect disruptive impulses and moods the propensity to suspend judgment—to think before acting	trustworthiness and integrity comfort with ambiguity openness to change
Motivation	a passion to work for reasons that go beyond money or status a propensity to pursue goals with energy and persistence	strong drive to achieve optimism, even in the face of failure organizational commitment
Empathy	the ability to understand the emotional makeup of other people skill in treating people according to their emotional reactions	expertise in building and retaining talent cross-cultural sensitivity service to clients and customers
Social Skill	proficiency in managing relationships and building networks an ability to find common ground and build rapport	effectiveness in leading change persuasiveness expertise in building and leading teams

I predict that emotional intelligence will become increasingly valuable as our society progresses with robotic technology. No matter how sophisticated technology gets, it will never be able to emulate the miracle of the human brain and its ability to demonstrate the traits listed above. But are we born with it, or can it be learned?

More from Goleman's article:

For ages, people have debated if leaders are born or made. So too goes the debate about emotional intelligence. Are people born with certain levels of empathy, for example, or do they actually acquire empathy as a result of life's experiences? The answer is both. Scientific inquiry strongly suggests that there is a genetic component to emotional intelligence. Psychological and developmental research indicates that nurture plays a role as well. How much of each will perhaps never be known, but research and practice clearly demonstrate that emotional intelligence can be learned.

Even better news? It increases with age. (Sorry, Millennials, we Gen X'ers are just more likeable than you!)

In another HBR article on the human economy,[12] author Dov Seidman states:

In the human economy, the most valuable workers will be hired hearts. The know-how and analytic skills that made them indispensable in the knowledge economy no longer give them an advantage over increasingly intelligent machines. But they will still bring to their work essential traits that can't be and won't be programmed into software, like creativity, passion, character, and collaborative spirit—their humanity, in other words. The ability to leverage these strengths will be the source of one organization's superiority over another. The companies that succeed best will be those that focus on the humanity of work, and capitalize on what humans can uniquely do.

---

12   Seidman, Dov, "From the Knowledge Economy to the Human Economy," *Economy, Harvard Business Review*, November 12, 2004, https://hbr.org/2014/11/from-the-knowledge-economy-to-the-human-economy.

In a guest post on my blog, Sandra Zorrati, marketing leader and author of the book *Precision Marketing: Maximizing Revenue through Relevance*, explains it this way:

> Customers today demand more depth, emotion, and personality from companies. As a result, it seems every brand is trying to be more "human" these days, but few are getting it right. We proclaim "customers first," change "we" to "you" on our corporate websites, and post a few heartwarming photos and videos. But that's not enough. In order to truly transform our brands, we must first look internally and cultivate highly human marketing leaders and teams.

Sandra also recommends these three points to be a more human leader:

1. ***Put emotion back into leadership.*** *We are emotional beings, and when we are moved we act. More importantly, if we are not moved, we ignore, we discard, we move on without hesitation.*
2. ***Be humble.*** *According to a* Catalyst *study,*[13] *humility is a critical leadership factor for creating an environment where employees feel included. When you admit mistakes, learn from criticism, don't pretend to have all of the answers, and empower your employees to learn and develop, your employees are more likely to feel included, innovative, and be willing to go above and beyond the call of duty.*
3. ***Champion people.*** *Put your employees at the center. Seek to understand them before asking them to understand you. Shining*

---

13 Catalyst Knowledge center. *Inclusive Leadership: The View From Six Countries Report*, 2014. http://www.catalyst.org/knowledge/inclusive-leadership-view-six-countries (accessed February 4, 2015).

the spotlight on others doesn't diminish your accomplishments—it actually makes them shine brighter.

So how does being more human translate into marketing? Forward-thinking companies do this with content marketing and social sharing, and they build in touchpoints of human interaction along the way. So let's talk about this content—what we share, how much we share. What's the optimum amount of giving before we can expect to get something in return?

The Giving Ratio

Marketers have long known that they need to give value before asking for a sale, and everyone has their own take on how much you should give before you get. For example, I firmly believe that reciprocity can't be forced; the minute you try to force a relationship is the minute that relationship weakens. More often than not, brands should adopt a give, give, give, give (and keep giving) mindset.

Gary Vaynerchuk, in his books *The Thank You Economy* and *Jab, Jab, Jab, Right Hook*, talks about the importance of changing your business mindset from always landing killer blows that result in immediate conversions and sales to focusing on making the customer happy. It takes patience to engage and build relationships—it's work, and it takes time. "We're primed for immediate gratification," he says in *Jab, Jab, Jab, Right Hook*. "… If we don't have to be patient, we won't." As with boxing, he says, success with marketing requires strategic thinking. The right hook gets all the credit for the win, but it's the ring movement and the series of well-planned jabs that come before it that set you up for success. Is there a specific formula for the number of jabs you have to deliver before you can execute that right hook? No. As with building any relationship, there isn't a set giving ratio that always gets results. People respond when they're ready.

My biggest pet peeve is when people tweet me out of the blue to ask for a review of their website, to support their campaign, to give them money—you get the picture. I'm a giving person, but I'm sorry, who are you again? That's like someone proposing to you after a handshake introduction. The same is true for business—trust needs to be built first; then your audience *wants* to help you succeed, instead of you as a brand having to ask them for an action. My friend Jay Baer, author of *Youtility*, says that when you're always helpful, you'll be the first place the receiver looks when they need something. Amen!

It's more important to develop a culture shift in your business to embrace a giving mindset than try to plan a hunting strategy. Ted Rubin, in his book *Return on Relationship*, states that marketing should be focused on *building relationships,* and metrics need to expand beyond ROI (return on investment) to include RonR: Return on Relationship™. No magic giving formula exists that always results in ROI, but if you change your entire outlook to one of helping and giving, you stand a much better chance of getting answers to your strategic calls to action along the way.

And sometimes numbers aren't the only success measurement. As marketers and business people, we've been trained to set our performance indicators, or metrics, as measureable "things." But as emotional intelligence becomes of greater value within business, we should be thinking about alternative ways to measure a successful interaction, employee retention, customer happiness, or even the effect of our unique culture on other businesses. I am willing to bet that Zappos's renowned approach to culture and customer satisfaction had a lot to do with Amazon wanting to acquire them. Sometimes a feeling, or the collective energy—or X-factor—within a business, has everything to do with its success.

My giving ratio formula: give as long as it feels good for me to do so. Maybe I won't get anything back right away, or perhaps not at all, but it feels good to keep giving anyway. I try to make it my primary focus. I encourage my employees to adopt a giving mindset as well (with each other and with our customers).

Will it be uncomfortable? Yes, at first, especially if you grew up with the phrase "Don't give away the store." To create shared experiences in the human economy, the old hoarding mindset just isn't going to work. The sooner you let go of it and embrace sharing as the way of doing business, the faster you'll see results. Building relationships and interacting with consumers on a human-to-human basis is the future of commerce.

Do People Trust What You're Sharing?

When it comes to trust, third-party and word-of-mouth sharing has always carried more weight than advertising, and the changes in search engine algorithms are reflecting that. In addition to content, these engines are now prioritizing what other people are sharing about you online. So it behooves brands to become their own media companies and curate in ways that facilitate conversation about their products and services.

Michael Brito describes this very well in his book *Your Brand: The Next Media Company*. In it he outlines the way brands and individuals need to adapt their content strategy to social sharing to create their own media platforms. Dell, for instance, has built a media platform that gives traditional news outlets a run for their money. Yahoo lured star reporters Katie Couric and David Pogue away from the networks to lend trusted faces to their new media platform. LinkedIn is building its own content network and inviting members to participate. The digital space is shifting emphasis away from broadcast and toward developing interesting content.

However, being your own publishing company isn't enough if you're talking about the same things as everyone else. To have the edge over your competition, you need to be the first out with your information. The good news is that the Web allows you to do that.

Tech evangelist and author Robert Scoble does this very well. He aims to be the first to discuss or introduce a technology topic and has become a respected thought leader as a result. He's a great example of a "give, give, give, give, give, get" personality.

Recently I attended Robert's fiftieth birthday party in Napa. It was a three-day event, complete with two hundred of his industry friends who were wine tasting, networking, and, most importantly, honoring Robert for the good work he's done over the years. He has built trust with his audience for what he shares. Robert, knowing that the high-powered Silicon Valley tech audience was there to see what he had in store, used his platform to help a few folks he cared about. He's a class act and has my eternal respect. At the main event on a Saturday night, he gave the spotlight to struggling artists performing for the first time, as well as winemaker Sarah Francis. Sarah has a dramatic story; without any formal training, she beat the odds by creating the top-ranked wine in Napa, but then lost a great deal of product in the Napa earthquake. Because of the platform Robert gave her and her heartfelt story, within a few weeks Sarah had secured full funding to take her wine production to the next level.

 Sarah Francis
Yesterday at 2:05pm · Napa, CA · 🔍

Just got a call from SFO they've landed and the LA and San Diego Meetings re Sarah Francis Proposal accepted -documents headed to 5 different legals and meet again Friday! Told Andy! I have more meetings everyday scheduled with other partners as well. Andy said "It's gonna be a great new year for you!!!"
Grapes are excited! I'm excited!!! Hallelujah! Heart is racing!!! Feet aren't touching the ground!

Unlike · Comment · Share · Buffer

👍 You, Chris Heuer, Kristie Wells, Robert Scoble and 148 others like this.

Being Delightful

Currently, I am kind of obsessed with In-N-Out Burger. For those of you outside California, In-N-Out Burger is a regional fast-food burger establishment with about five things on their menu: burgers, cheeseburgers, French fries, onion rings, and milkshakes. How do they compete with so many other fast-food burger joints, especially in health-conscious California? Their ingredients are basically the same, so what makes them so competitive? Do they make a better burger?

As any In-N-Out Burger-brand loyal customer knows, all their burgers come with a special sauce somewhat similar to Thousand Island dressing. But their real "special sauce" lies in their business model, which hasn't changed in over three decades since they opened their doors. According to their model, In-N-Out Burger exists for the purpose of:

1. Providing the freshest, highest-quality foods and services for a profit and a spotless, sparkling environment whereby the customer is our most important asset.
2. Providing a team-oriented atmosphere whereby goal-setting and communications exist and providing excellent training and development for all of our associates.
3. Assisting all communities in our marketplace to become stronger, safer and better places to live.

Their special sauce—simple but clear business objectives—has kept them focused and has built a solid brand that keeps people coming back. That, and their delicious burgers.

How they delight their customers is in their secret, unpublished menu. At least it was for years. Recently I learned they now list it on their menu as a "not-so-secret" menu. But even still, you won't find these menu items on the print menu. You have to search online to find other fans who have learned exactly what you *can* order, then get the intel from them. This is delight through sharing—a brand that knows its customers and gives them something special, and those customers in turn share it with others to extend the experience. Brilliant!

The Power of Humor

Being human means we need to laugh at ourselves sometimes. Laughter is where we all find the most commonality—because we're happy together. Humor creates moments when we just sit and think, and it takes our minds off of things that are not going so well or are challenging. Making fun of life and the things that weigh us down relieves us; it simply feels great to laugh!

Brand experiences built around happiness and joy aren't new— we've been developing them since the *Mad Men* days. It's important to take that concept into sharing because it allows us to create magical moments—the kind that cement the idea in our customers' minds that we're fun to be around. Who wants to be known as a brand that's always serious? We all want to be human brands and relaxed enough to laugh at ourselves once in a while.

"Humor is a complex cognitive process akin to creativity," says Mitch Earleywine, PhD, professor of psychology at SUNY Albany in an interview with iMedia Connection.[14] "That means marketers can use humor to improve their moods, memories, and problem-solving abilities—not to mention their levels of innovation. Furthermore, humor is a core interpersonal skill for enhancing relationships—and that has everything to do with how marketers persuade and encourage loyalty among customers."

Humor is an essential element to being more human online because it's another way that we connect with others in real life. People have

---

14   Leuchtefeld, Lori. "How to harness the marketing power of humor," *iMedia Connection* (blog). http://www.imediaconnection.com/content/28675. asp#b4raLCtvdG0VvlDf.99]

shared humorous situations since the beginning of time and via all forms of communication. When employed in the right context and as a part of your planned content strategy, humor can cement bonds, ease tension, even help smooth the way for collaboration. As with other types of content, both context and timing are important. So experiment and find the best mix for you or your company, but don't leave humor out—it's an essential part of being human.

Humor is how I connect with others the most on Facebook. I like to entertain my friends there and make them laugh, so if I ever need to gather some real research, I'll have an army of people willing to give back. Recently I posted this after reading about Mazda's marketing slogan in a trade article (because it totally made me laugh):

Bryan Kramer
23 hrs · San Jose, CA · ◉

Mazda's marketing slogan is "We Build Mazdas." They decided on it after rejecting others like: "Mazdas Are Cars" and "Buy Mazdas With Money"

Like · Comment · Share · Buffer

👍 Krista Pratt Valpreda, Scott Carter, Todd Wilms and 59 others like this.

Todd Wilms "You'll never get laid with this car" was a close second.
23 hrs · Like · 👍 4

Vincent Orleck "Mazda: It Starts With An M."

"We Build Mazdas, And Occasionally Sell Them."

"Looking For A Vehicle With 4 Wheels And An Engine? Think Mazda."
23 hrs · Like · 👍 1

Rajesh Setty 🙂
17 hrs · Like · 👍 1

Brian Guest Laughing out loud
8 hrs · Like · 👍 1

Carol Gray Funny!
6 hrs · Like · 👍 1

Chris Brogan I love your sense of humor very much.
2 hrs · Like

Steve Woodruff "It almost rhymes with Kwanzaa, but not really."
2 hrs · Like

Mazda's marketing slogan is "We Build Mazdas." They decided on it after rejecting others like: "Mazdas Are Cars" and "Buy Mazdas With Money"

The post got hilarious responses!

Apparently, I'm friends on Facebook with many others who get my sense of humor. As a personal brand, that's critical to why people share my content in other platforms. There's a lot of overlap of the same people on different platforms, and they all work together.

My business partner and wife, Courtney Smith, also uses humor across her social channels. Her style is different, however. She prefers to comment on other people's posts with a funny comeback or observation, as opposed to posting herself. Typically she posts sarcastic rants, photos of friends and family, or shares articles she finds interesting or relevant to someone in her network. She loves to entertain as I do, but you can see it's possible to achieve this in different ways. The key is consistency, authenticity, and frequency; don't drop off the earth because people forget fast.

Quantity + Quality x Consistency = Success

In the end, the drive to be more responsive to our audiences and stay connected to them means that we are constantly producing content. Our customers are demanding more from us as marketers, so whether it's humorous, delightful, thought provoking, or informative, we need to publish content constantly.

Brands like Nestle are investing in this "blanketing" of content on social channels in a big way, spending upwards of $127,000 per day on Facebook posts alone. However, I feel strongly that if you're missing any one of the legs of the formula—quantity, quality, or consistency—you won't be successful no matter how much you spend.

Rising above the noise is a big challenge, but it's not just about delivering quantity, it's also about delivering quality—and doing both consistently. You can't depend on one piece of content going viral; you have to share good stories consistently across multiple channels, and all of it must be geared to your audience.

In the direct mail era, marketers faced the same challenges in getting their content to rise to the top and be noticed. Those who experienced the most success used the same formula: multiple pieces of quality content mailed on a consistent basis. But in today's transmedia world, this formula also applies to our interactions with the individuals who consume our content. Our job shifts from producing content to creating experiences through engagement with that content. Bringing human connection into the equation requires the same dedication to frequency, quality of contact, and consistency, and success is measured by how much these experiences with our brands are shared.

PART II
THE -OLOGY OF SHARING

The study of sharing requires us to look at the concept from all sides—as an action, intent, philosophy, plan, and creative exercise. There are many facets of sharing—setting up your strategy, taking a deeper look at influence and how to cultivate it, talking with platform experts and breaking down the mechanics of it, for instance—to deconstruct and understand.

Doing so also includes the study of *how* it all works together.

DISCLAIMER

Part II of Shareology *is pretty "in the weeds." This is everything I've learned about social sharing, so take from it what's useful and skip over the rest if you already know it. Or tweet me your perspective, because I too am always learning.* ☺

What does it really mean to be connected as a company? There are lots of airy theories out there, but unless you can attach real strategy to them, they aren't going to provide a whole lot of value. That's where scientific measurement changes everything. If you're in business to make money (and most of us are), you can't have a sharing strategy that doesn't include measurement and analytics. A lot of CEOs have data scientists on their teams who research and tell them what they need, but I've always loved doing that for myself. I like to explore and analyze, and on average I get one or two requests every week to test new pieces of software. I've tested, skilled, and optimized just about every piece of social analytic software that's been given to me because without the science side, you really don't know what's going on around you and where you should be concentrating.

For example, if I hadn't used social listening software, I would never have known the true reach of my first book, *H2H*, because many people didn't associate it with me. If I were listening just for attribution (which only happened about a third of the time), I would assume the book was just doing okay. However, because I used listening software, I could tell within the first forty-eight hours of its release that *H2H* got over 80 million impressions. There's no way I could have seen that without understanding that data. It informed me to leverage the opportunity to write that book and release it with confidence, knowing people would want to learn more about the topic.

The facets of sharing live together in harmony are much like the yin/yang symbol. Technology supports social listening for opportunities, passing information into our brains so we can create great content in response to those opportunities. We can also use technology to amplify the message and measure the impact of what we shared.

In this book's introduction, I talked about a pivotal moment when I had a personal identity crisis relating to my business—that I had managed to delegate so well I didn't "connect" with my own company and felt like quitting. It's something that I was able to speak about again at a TED talk in 2014, thanks to IBM. I asked the audience:

> Can you imagine building a company that you want to leave? That left me thinking, "How can I connect? How can I connect back with my company—with myself? Who am I? What's my brand?"

Many of us ask the same questions of ourselves and of our companies, right? But reinventing yourself (or your brand) isn't something you can just do overnight. I found over time that sharing other people's stories without asking for anything in return helped their brand and broadened my own audience. The more I connected with other people and shared, the more my own messages began to resonate—something that was brought home to me when I spoke at Bloomberg West in San Francisco and shared the following message onstage, well before my TED opportunity:

There is no more B2B or B2C: It's H2H: Human-to-Human."

While I was onstage with that message behind me, people were raising their phones and taking pictures of the screen! What they were hearing meant something to them. But more than that, it was also resonating with people beyond the conference. We tracked the phrase and the hashtag #H2H over the next forty-eight hours and were shocked by the results: over eighty million impressions. It was also translated into more than fifteen languages and mentioned in over one thousand blogs during the next two weeks.

That experience was so exciting that I decided to conduct a live experiment during my TED talk (something that as far as I know was never done before). I told the audience:

I want every single person in this audience to experience the power of sharing through a live experiment. So take out your phone or your tablet right now. What I want you to do is take a look at the screen behind me.

I want you to take a picture of this and tweet out YOUR idea that could change the world. Don't think too hard on this ... it could be small—as simple as a smile to someone you haven't smiled at in a while. It can be a handshake. It can be a kind gesture, or it could be as large as solving world peace. Whatever your idea—whatever inspires you to share—I want you to share that now.

I did the same thing onstage, taking a picture and typing in the hashtag #sharinginspires, and tweeted "The power of sharing reimagined my future."

After a lunch break we came back and did it again then shared our results. By the end of the day, in just 4 hours, this hashtag had measured close to twenty-one million impressions, and the hashtag #sharinginspires trended number one nationally on Twitter. The ripple effect spread outside the conference across the world with tweets from the UK, India, South Africa, Japan, and Australia, in addition to the US.

Some of the ideas shared in these tweets were serious—others funny or inspiring. A few tweets that rang loudly for me were:

"What if we had a no-device rule at the dinner table every night?"

"It would be awesome if you pushed the pizza button on the microwave [and] a pizza actually came out."

"Using big data to analyze kidnapping and trafficking in person."

Conducting these two experiments reinforced my belief in the power of sharing and inspired me to dig even deeper for more understanding. What are the mechanics of sharing? How can businesses and individuals learn to replicate the process of sharing to build their brands? What are the necessary building blocks?

CHAPTER 5

SHARING: A SENSORY EXPERIENCE

No matter how we share, everything is communicated through body or verbal language. We use language to convey sensory experiences (what we see, hear, taste, or touch), and that hasn't changed since human communication began. What has evolved is the actual language we use to convey those experiences. Words and meanings have been changing for centuries, and within each of those changes, there were historical and contextual changes that altered the way humans interacted.

Today is no different. We have new acronyms like LOL, OMG, TY, or BRB, and words like selfie, hashtag, and Wiki. Some are new words (like selfie) while others (like hashtag) have a new "assigned" meaning in social context, but each has helped us converse in a new way. In quick statements, letters, and sometimes pictures, we're learning to speak a new language. With the advent of Twitter and texting, full, proper sentences are becoming a thing of the past because these formats are forcing us to communicate more efficiently. The faster we move online and with mobile devices, the more we will see language continue to change.

Brands need to become students of social linguistics—an essential part of sharing—to stay competitive. Social language is changing the shape of modern communication, just like other changes affected communication in the past. However, the social language evolution is happening faster, more disruptively, and with greater global context than ever before.

Understanding Your Social Body Language

Think about how you share, why you share, and what you've shared on social channels over the last month. We all share things differently because we see things through the "me" lens. However, how we perceive ourselves typically differs from how others see us, which in large part is determined by the collective language of what and how we share, and also who we share with online.

According to the *Forbes* article "Busting 5 Body Language Myths," a whopping 93 percent of communication is based on nonverbal body language.[15] That's huge! Picking up on body language cues when communicating in person is a skill that requires hands-on learning and practice. But what happens when those body cues, voice, tone, and demeanor disappear? How do we translate body language in social communications?

One of the most incredible things happening on the social Web right now is the development of social body language. When you're face-to-face with another person, subtle cues, such as a sarcastic tone, a hand gesture, or a twinkle in the eye, provide context for what's being said.

---

15 Goman, Carol Kinsey. "Busting 5 Body Language Myths." *Forbes Leadership (blog)*. http://www.forbes.com/sites/carolkinseygoman/2012/07/24/busting-5-body-language-myths/

However, divining what people mean when they're saying something in 140 characters or less, say, on Twitter, without these cues is much more difficult. Without your physical body language as a guide, the reader's current emotional state and circumstances are going to have much more influence on their perception of your written words.

Now think about brands. It's always been their mission to align their voice and values with their audience's values so they can communicate in a way that builds rapport; this is the sweet spot we've all been trying to reach as marketers, and it has always been a challenge. If marketers could really understand the social body language of their customers— if they could craft personalized words they know would resonate and deliver them at the right place and right time—they could build individualized relationships with customers online like never before. So why aren't we doing it?

One answer is lack of contextual data. Up until now, it has been hard to gather enough psychographic and social habit information online to fully identify our social customers and understand their social body language. Yes, there was lots of data out there, but combing through it all was problematic. Theoretically, the social Web has been around long enough so that companies and social platforms should be able to tell what you share, click on, and say simply by reviewing your habits and consistency in how and what you share.

I'm not saying this to scare you, because if brands truly wanted to target one person out of a billion, they wouldn't be making money on maximizing their efforts. But the truth is that if marketers could really understand their customers, they could build individualized relationships with them for their brands in a way like never before. Unfortunately, the easy analysis part of combing through all the big data has been challenging and not yet achieved. Even with all the analytics and tools at our fingertips, computer methodology could never quite get the true you—until now.

IBM Social Business has developed its own social software called "System U" that visually analyzes and categorizes into personality traits the entire body of an individual Twitter account. At a demo of the product at South by Southwest (SXSW), I used it to analyze my own social persona, social behavior, values, and needs, and it came up with some interesting traits.

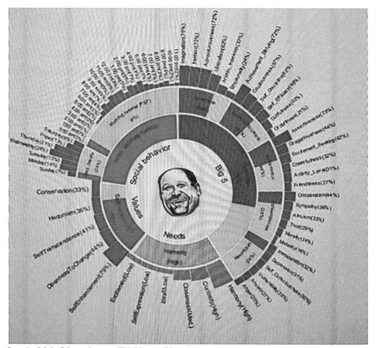

[caption] *My @bryankramer IBM SystemU analysis*

My @bryankramer IBM SystemU analysis

According to the analysis, I share more frequently on Wednesday morning at 11 a.m. over any other day or time. It told me I am someone who is giving and open, with a high level of harmony. These traits resonated with me because I could see how the outside world might perceive me in my own social body language. As a marketer, I started to realize how this could alter the way companies might speak to me. Would they have more success reaching me if they knew I was online Wednesday mornings at 11 a.m.? If they phrased a tweet to me using sentences like "We know you're open to new opportunities ..." or "Our crowd has been waiting for you ...," would I be more likely to engage because my own personality traits aligned with the language they used with me? Yes, I believe I would.

We all learned the mechanics of communication, manners, and sharing with others by observing and copying our parents, teachers, and peers. Learning the nuances and unspoken cues of body language, knowing when and what to share (as well as when and what not to share), is something we seem to instinctively "pick up" from childhood, and it gets tweaked by our experiences as we grow. Some people are naturally gifted at it. Some have to work harder to "get" it, and some have no aptitude for it at all. But there's no doubt that learning the art of reading another person's body language, tone, and expression greatly impacts the success or failure of one-on-one human communication.

To help your audience visualize your body language through a positive lens, you'll have to find other ways to add context. Social body language is how you interact online without the context of your offline behavior, so using things like photos, videos, and other interesting things can help create that context. It's well known that the visual components of the social Web are more interesting and spread faster than a text-only tweet or update.

Another way to do that is to build a positive image by always over-delivering, whether it's tweeting useful, enjoyable content, giving the unexpected attention or response, or in going the extra mile to provide value in your product or services. Your social audience is filtering the content they choose to read in their newsfeeds based on its value to them, period. So your overarching goal should be to share things that will matter to their lives. Be on the lookout for ways to surprise and delight your audience with unexpected value and connection on a steady basis.

Early Lessons in Delivering Value

I hated every single job I had in high school and college because they were always trying to get me to do something I thought was either being done the wrong way, or wasn't a process that enhanced the company. In one of the jobs, I had to make sandwiches in thirty seconds or less. Now if you took a look at those sandwiches after thirty seconds you'd say, "There's no way I'm eating that." Frustrated with this, I asked if we could make them in a minute, so people would actually *enjoy* the sandwiches. But nope, that wasn't part of the rule set.

In college, I was a delivery driver for Domino's Pizza. I loved that company and worked for them longer than any other while I was in school. I wore the hat and proudly flew the Domino's flag from my 1984 blue Chevy Blazer. The job had a huge downside, however: the tips were dismal. One day while I was shopping at Safeway, I noticed a palette of Coke and Diet Coke on sale for a quarter for a two-liter. Bells and whistles went off in my head! I bought the whole palette and loaded up the back of my Blazer.

Now, on my deliveries, I was typically greeted at the door by a broke, most likely stoned college student who never had ANY extra money, so tips were nonexistent. But after my fateful Safeway visit, with every medium or large pizza order, I would hand my customers a two-liter bottle—for free. They would look at me every time and say, "Dude ... I didn't order that," to which I replied, "No problem—I figured you'd be thirsty while you ate your pizza, so it's on me." Talk about a turnaround in my tips! I would get huge smiles and people reaching deep into their pockets for ones, fives, even ten-dollar bills! They would find the money because I was delivering value to them. From that point forward, I realized that when I gave as much value as I could, I could change the outcome in my favor. And indeed, my outcome—and INCOME— changed. As I continued to give those two liters of Coke to the customers, my nightly tips rose to about $400 or $500. As a twenty-year-old college student, I was living large.

Then, a month and a half later, the jig was up. I got called into the delivery station office. Here's how the conversation went:

Manager: "We have a problem, Bryan ... we've been getting calls that people aren't receiving their two-liters from the other drivers."

Me: "Well, maybe they should ask for me then."

Manager: "You have to stop giving away free two-liters. It's not a Domino's promotion, and you're not allowed to do it."

Me: "Well, you really should be doing it, so all the drivers can make more tips."

Manager: "No."

Me: "Okay, well, I guess then I should find somewhere else that appreciates the concept of value."

So I turned in my hat and flag. Being penalized for giving value? That's not how I wanted to do business with people. Recently I got a chance to meet the head of social media for Domino's and told him that story. He laughed and said they actually ran that as a promotion sometime in the late '90s, so of course I will take full credit for giving them the idea!

Those early lessons in giving value primed me to translate them into digital communications today—to make it part of my personal brand. That's what social media is really about—building your own brand by creating a social body language that mirrors your values and allows you to deliver something useful to your audience. The graphic below shows how social body language mirrors physical body language in four key areas:

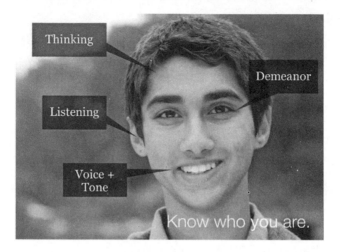

These four areas from your physical world can be built into your brand online with authenticity and transparency so your audience knows exactly who you are.

Listening: The Big Daddy of Social Body Language

If there's one thing we should all practice more, it's listening. None of us do it enough. There are huge opportunities here because most brands are totally missing the boat. An overwhelming majority (85 percent according to Social Media Explorer) are not listening to consumer feedback online, and more than two-thirds (Loyalty 360 says 70 percent) aren't even collecting social media data about their competitors. Smart brands collect this kind of data, actively listen, and (most importantly) engage with their social audiences. As a result they have a big advantage over their competitors who open platforms and never use them for anything other than spewing content.

Gleaning actionable information from escalating online babble requires a comprehensive strategy and structure. Without it, you're just scattered, looking at data everywhere. So what's your company's *why*? Are you looking for more sales? Are you seeking ways to reduce churn? Do you want better collaboration with partners? More productivity from your employees? Once you crystallize your *why*, you'll laser focus on the right audience, listening tools, and engagement strategy. Goals first, listening second.

A good illustration of a customer service *why* is Naked Wines. For fellow oenophiles, Naked Wines enables first-time or boutique winemakers to produce and distribute their product at much lower cost by decreasing their overhead and crowdsourcing the funding for production from Angels, or the members of their wine consortium. Recently Courtney and I went to a Naked Wines local event and ordered a shipment of wine. State law requires that someone over twenty-one be home to sign for the delivery. Well, unfortunately for us, the delivery service kept trying to deliver the wine while we were at work, between 9 a.m. and 6 p.m. Three times we missed the delivery (even though we continually wrote on the delivery notices sticky-noted to our front door to please come between 6 and 8 p.m.).

It got frustrating. Calls to the third-party delivery service customer service line resulted in hang-ups, misdirection, and unsympathetic customer service agents offering no solution other than us driving the two-hour trek to Sonoma to pick up the box. Finally, Courtney tweeted out to the head of sales of the delivery service: "I can't believe @NakedWines [delivery service] is not listening! I have a full-time job … all I'm asking is [that] they come 30 minutes later!" Not only did the woman reply to Courtney's tweet, she proactively looked up our order using Courtney's name, got her cell phone number, and called her personally to schedule the delivery for 6:30 the next day.

Done. The delivery service was listening, and lucky for them, averted losing a customer.

Assuming you have your *why* figured out, what's next in the listening process? There are a billion and a half tweets in the Twitter stream every two days. Where do you start? Rather than searching for hashtags, start with your ideal audience. Once you're clear on your objectives and who you want to do business with, then you can pick appropriate listening tools and set them up.

Social Listening Tools

Just a few short years ago the only tool we had for listening online was Google Alerts. Now contextual technologies are being developed faster than you can say "big data." A plethora of tools can parse the river of conversation on any network—we recommend Social Report, Hootsuite, Mutual Mind, Sprinklr, or SpiderQube; we use them all. They can discover who's saying what about anything, where they are on the globe when they're saying it, context, sentiment, shoe size—you name it—and spit back out what's useful to you in whatever form you need it.

For instance, we worked with a global tier-one culinary school to listen across the social Web to identify new student opportunities. Instead of just plugging the word "Food" into our social listening system, which would have returned too many meaningless results, we used the long-tail keyword term "I want to become a chef." It narrowed our interest focus, and we discovered that "I want to become a chef" was mentioned every 51 seconds on Twitter, returning 1,639 results (on average) a day.

Looking at how that phrase performed, we learned that in March its shares spiked big time to over 10,000. Why the jump from 1,639? Turns out a farm-to-table press release went out on that day, which proved that public relations played a big role in driving social interest and engagement on Twitter for this subject. This kind of information was invaluable, because it showed our client where they could smartly spend their future marketing dollars and the potential power of how two channels could work together to be stronger than they were alone.

Software is just software, however, and doesn't add value unless you have an informed team and know where you're going with the data you're pulling. You need to run at least a month of data, otherwise you have nothing to compare against. Are you listening to the right keywords? Are you optimizing the right thing? Is it generating the right results? Are you tagging your results and categorizing them across your business operations?

Listening can touch every aspect of your organization, internally and externally, so setting up your tools properly to line up with your objectives is important—as well as picking the right people for a listening team.

Build the Right Listening Team

According to Exact Target's report "2014 State of Marketing,"[16] 60 percent of marketers surveyed used social listening strategies in 2013, but only 31 percent thought their social listening was effective. Why aren't businesses getting better results? Two of the biggest reasons might be 1) not dedicating enough resources and 2) handing the process to the wrong person (or persons). Every social business should dedicate more than just one person to their social listening strategy and build a team. In fact, we form teams (small pods) at PureMatter for every client engagement: a listening analyst, a social engagement specialist, and a social media manager who all work in tandem. You need the big picture people and the in-the-trenches people working together to make sure

16   Salesforce, Exacttarget Marketing Cloud. *2014 State of Marketing.* http://content.exacttarget.com/en/StateOfMarketing2014?ls=Website&lss= StateofMarketing2014&lssm=Corporate&camp=701A0000000g98RIAQ (accessed February 6, 2015).

everything's getting tended to, because it takes more than one skill set to get this done.

One brand that has built a great listening system and team is American Airlines. A lot of social media activity is generated around the airlines every week (forty-two thousand mentions on Twitter alone), so how do they keep up with it all? Their solution of choice is a Social Command Center from MutualMind. The Command Center offers deep analytics to help the airline zero in on content that matters to them and powerful data visualization tools like tag clouds and heat maps to help social team members make sense of the data. They can monitor regions across the globe, spot breaking trends, track mentions and images—even engage customers and cross-functional customer care teams directly. Visualizing this deep listening, monitoring sentiment and creating timelier responses is extremely powerful (even essential). It allows American to measure the overall effectiveness of their customer service across the social sphere and make adjustments quickly, something that was impossible just a few short years ago.

One of the most phenomenal examples of team building is Social Media Examiner (SME). The founder of SME, Michael Stelzner, gave us the lowdown on his strategy for building a cohesive team.

The first step in building a good team is having a corporate vision statement. Our corporate vision statement is "Social Media Examiner is the world's largest and most respected provider of social media marketing content. We are known for our popular articles, reports, podcasts, webinars, summits, and in-person events. In our active community, we always strive for excellence in all we do."

That statement is distributed across everyone that works for us, and we train everyone in what we call Nordstrom-quality service. Every member of our team, whether they are servicing employees, customers, prospects, or online people, is to provide the kind of experience you would expect if you walked into a Nordstrom store, which means you go to them before they need help.

If they see someone at a physical conference looking bewildered, they walk up and ask how they can help them, and then walk them where they need to go. They monitor all of our social channels for people that are asking questions.

It also means doing things like staffing people on our Facebook wall around the clock to answer questions that people have about social media. We actually pay personnel to answer any and all questions that people post on our Facebook wall about anything related to social. If we don't know the answer we find someone in our network who does, and we ask them to come answer that question. That's what I call the Nordstrom level of service. The only way to be able to pull that off with teams is to make sure that everybody buys in and everybody understands what it means.

We're still a small company, not a big brand. We have a big footprint in the world of social media marketing, but we're not a mega corporation, so it's a very limited team that's trained. We try our best to make sure that every question gets answered in a relatively quick period of time.

Listening is another thing the SME team is trained to do in preparation for our online events, and a live chatbox opens on the registration page that says, "Can I answer any questions for you?" They have scripts behind the scenes with common questions, and the answers to those questions.

People on our team also monitor the event hashtag around the clock and answer questions on various social channels—again armed with scripted answers to the most common questions. We've identified all of the places where people ask questions, and [we] assign personnel that are capable and trained to answer those kinds of questions.

Time is of the essence when it comes to this kind of service. In the end, we know that these are all prospects that may be buying, so we know that it's important that we answer those questions quickly.

How do we keep team members from bumping into each other? A bit of technology comes in handy. With our live support agents, the technology we use is called SnapEngage, which synchronizes with Skype. It finds all of the available agents and automatically assigns a particular agent. If, for whatever reason, that agent needs to pass a question on to another person, it sends it on to that other person.

Everything is recorded, and we have a different team that looks at how those questions were answered, how fast they were answered. Whether it's a question on Twitter, Facebook or LinkedIn, we can see publicly if it has not been addressed. We also have people assigned to different responsibilities that generally don't overlap, and they're distributed across the world to cover different time slots.

Because listening is such an important component in today's world, leading-edge companies are creating their own listening systems and establishing dedicated teams to run them. For instance, the managed cloud company Rackspace built their own social media listening tools that let them find conversations (about them and their competitors), tag them, assign them to other team members, keep track of trends over time, and follow up on responses.

Whatever tools you end up using, as long as you're measuring the right things you can definitely equate the rise or fall of results with your bottom line. But ROI is more than just a campaign-based marketing metric. Selling, loyalty, customer retention, content creation—all business processes get much easier when everyone listens, measures, and then takes action based on what they hear.

The Importance of *Active* Listening

It's the conversation on any platform that gives you real value, and that requires not just listening for data, but actively listening, which is still a rare human practice. Active listening means truly paying attention and engaging effectively based on the context of a digital conversation. It's the next step in social listening. It's looking at the twenty-five thousand active conversations that happen in a given time period and zeroing in on one where you can respond and make a difference. The question everyone monitoring those listening posts should ask themselves is: How can I help? When we listen to find and offer solutions to solving problems on a personal level, we're in a whole new realm, and it's a game changer.

Using your listening tool of choice helps you find that needle in the haystack, and the social haystack is huge. There are 350,000 new tweets and over 500,000 new Facebook comments every minute! Active listening means empowering your teams with these tools so they can engage with your fans in a timely and relevant manner; customer care is a great example of this kind of opportunity.

Brands that practice active listening can reap big dividends in loyalty and advocacy. I had an experience with a car rental company that provides a clear example of this. What happened? In a tweet, I lamented the fact that I had accidentally left my iPad in a Hertz rental car after I returned it. Next thing I knew, a Hertz representative was reaching out to me. He'd seen my lament on Twitter! Within a few business days, I was informed that my iPad had been found and it was returned to me. That experience not only won Hertz a customer for life, but also created advocacy they couldn't buy with an ad or a promotion.

Here's another example: I was flying Virgin America and tweeted about how excited I was to have a hot cup of coffee, WiFi, and an electrical outlet in the sky on my way to my IBM conference. Virgin was actively listening on social media, and two minutes later via Twitter, their community manager not only thanked me for the shout-out but also wished me a great time in Orlando. The remarkable thing about this was that *I never mentioned Orlando in my earlier tweet.* Their community manager put two and two together, knowing their flight hubs and the conference I referenced, to know that I was on my way there. So they used this information to personalize their response. That's active listening—going the extra mile to respond quickly and to personalize the conversation. This one tweet response turned into over two hundred retweets within an hour and two blogs written by complete strangers on the subject, all before I landed in Orlando. I would guess that Virgin probably earned about two million impressions on this just because they were actively listening. At Twitter's average CPM of $3.50/thousand impressions for paid social, that one interaction would have cost about $7,000. Worth it? I'd say absolutely.

The benefits of active listening aren't limited to companies with big budgets, however. Individuals can benefit as well, even C-suite executives! Vala Afshar, the CMO of the IT networks provider Extreme Networks, relates the story of active listening success when he was just a newly minted CMO with no social media experience.

.ıl. AT&T 4G   7:53 PM   ⌁ ⋇ 65% ⬛

Connect   **Tweet**   ✎

Amber Close @CloseAmber   6h
Social Buzz at #IBMConnect - @BryanKramer CEO PureMatter - How Social Listening is best kept secret Tues 1 pm Social Cafe

Bryan Kramer @bryankramer   💬 6h
Can't wait @CloseAmber, flying to #IBMConnect now on greatest airline @virginamerica with internet, electricity and great service. #wow :-)

Virgin America
@VirginAmerica

@bryankramer Thanks for the shout. Have a great time in #Orlando.
1/27/13, 5:00 PM

Our CIO set me up with a Twitter account in 2011 and told me I should be using it. Not knowing the first thing about Twitter, I agreed to try it for a month, but in just ten days I was hooked. At first I just curated other people's content that I thought would be valuable to other executives, but I soon found it invaluable for reaching out to collaborate on content creation. For example, I've often floated a question on Twitter asking if any CIOs or CMOs would like to coauthor a blog post on a specific industry topic, and people very generously respond. I've been generated a lot of content that way. I've found that the other executives who are active on Twitter and actively listening often volunteer to help.

Vala's experience with other executives on Twitter highlights the value of sharing expertise, especially if you're willing to listen and look for those opportunities.

The main goal of active listening on social channels shouldn't be to sell someone something, but to help someone get something done, says social media author Shel Israel, who coauthored two books with Robert Scoble, *Naked Conversations* and *The Age of Context*. However, Shel lamented to me that many marketers still don't understand this concept.

When I talk to marketers, their focus seems automatically to shift to "When a customer is nearby, I can push something out at them," which is absolutely the wrong approach. If they interrupt the flow of the data points of who, what, when, where, and why, then they'll lose the relationship by pushing out stuff. If you just wait [and listen], you'll know that a customer is building a deck. And that deck requires lag screws that the person has not yet purchased. Now you can approach them and say, "Hey, Bryan. Good to see you again. How's the deck coming? Did you need lag screws for the project or benches? I'll be happy to answer any questions." Becoming a helper and facilitator is a huge advantage. But like most bad salespeople, marketers just won't shut up and listen.

Every day we are presented with opportunities to create positive interactions with customers, collaborate with peers, and correct potentially costly mistakes if we'll just listen for them. Don't skimp on it, because people have more power and influence on others than you may realize, and what you don't know can (and often does) hurt you.

Voice and Tone

In my first chapter of *H2H* I talked about the "Unnatural Language of Business" and how we all need to learn to "speak more human" in our content and interactions with people. Social has brought with it a whole new iteration of language, and each platform has its own nuances; but how does social language influence what we share in social communities and how other people interpret it? Where is language heading?

It all boils down to understanding the language of the community. Humans naturally seek out communities of likeminded people to share experiences, and from a linguistics standpoint, there are lots of interesting things to look at concerning real-life and online communities. For one thing, we tend to form real-life communities around geographic constraints, whereas online we have the ability to reach anyone, anywhere in the world. Our social connection possibilities are much deeper now because of the Internet, which has a rich effect on our cultural identities, our general knowledge base, and even our language.

Every day, thanks to the Internet, new words get adopted into common speech. For instance, everyone understands "friending" someone on Facebook, even if they don't use Facebook. There are terms exclusive to Twitter or Tumblr that leak into our speech (and eventually the dictionary), like "hashtag" or "gif," or the shortening acronyms like TBH (to be honest) or IMHO (in my humble opinion). When you start to see people in those communities adopting these linguistic clues, it's basically a signal that states, "I'm part of this community, and I speak the way this group speaks."

Does changing social language affect how and what we share? According to Lera Boroditsky, an assistant professor of psychology, neuroscience, and symbolic systems at Stanford University, studies on language in different countries illustrate how language shapes thought. One of her articles[17] published in Edge.org examines this, but her summation shows how language affects the way we perceive (and ultimately share) information:

> ... studies have found effects of language on how people construe events, reason about causality, keep track of numbers, understand material substance, perceive and experience emotion, reason about other people's minds, choose to take risks, and even in the way they choose professions and spouses. Taken together, these results show that linguistic processes are pervasive in most fundamental domains of thought, unconsciously shaping us from the nuts and bolts of cognition and perception to our loftiest abstract notions and major life decisions. Language is central to our experience of being human, and the languages we speak profoundly shape the way we think, the way we see the world, the way we live our lives.

Demeanor

Projecting the same demeanor on social channels day in and day out gets boring quickly, and you'll lose your audience's trust. It's like getting

17   Boroditsky, Lera. "How Does Our Language Shape The Way We Think?" *Edge Conversations.* http://edge.org/conversation/how-does-our-language-shape-the-way-we-think (accessed February 6, 2015).

stuck next to someone at a cocktail party who talks about the same things over and over. Loosening up a bit and looking for something different to share makes you and/or your brand more interesting and fun to be around. Sharing things that are a little quirky or funny once in a while reveals your human side, especially relaying stories about your experiences that people can relate to their own lives—or not.

I once relayed a story on Facebook about meeting some *Star Wars* characters on the sidewalk in Vegas as I walked from my hotel to CES. Darth Vader, Chewbacca, and a Storm Trooper stood outside the show entrance, and Darth, who spotted me, asked me if I would take a picture

with them. Heck yeah! So I took the picture, and almost immediately after, the Storm Trooper leaned over and said something to Chewbacca that he clearly didn't like … and Chewbacca decked him! Suddenly it turned into an all-out fistfight, the two characters writhing on the ground. I was too stunned to do anything but stare, and as Darth Vader and I stood there watching the brawl,

he leaned over to me and in his Darthy stage voice muttered, "Sch-h-h-h-h—ch [breathing in and out sound] … I've had it with these two." Who does that? The moment was just too good not to share.

My demeanor online is a combination of funny, irreverent, informative, and supporting my fellow peers by sharing their content. A blend keeps things interesting.

Concentrating on building these skills will help you develop a social body language that allows your fans to relate to you in a much more meaningful (and human) way. The more you concentrate on just being human in social conversations and creating and sharing content that you and your audiences care about, the more value your brand will accrue, and the more productive your social relationships will be.

CHAPTER 6

TIMING IS EVERYTHING

I t's critical that we all practice timing when and what we share. Knowing when to say (or not to say) something can make a huge difference in our relationships. How many times during a conversation have you thought, *Gee, I wish I had known this earlier? ...* or *Wow, what were they thinking?* Not the best time or place to share that ... timing is everything.

The best communicators know how to time what they say to coincide with when their audience is most receptive, whether that's in online or offline conversations. There's no difference.

Test When You Share

So when is the perfect time to share content with your audience? You can find the answer by testing your posts to see what resonates and when. Here again, the science of listening is helpful and can change your results dramatically. For example, I used to set my tweets to release between 6 a.m. and 10 p.m., which led to what I considered good engagement. But when I analyzed all my Twitter follower activity, I found out that I was missing engagement from 1 a.m. to 4 a.m., which correlated to when my European audience was sharing. So I tweaked my schedule to release tweets between those hours. When I ran the report again two weeks later, the results were off the charts! Over half of my Twitter audience hailed from European time zones, and the engagement during that 1 to 4 a.m. slot was double what I received during the day.

I also found that Saturday was a slow day for my audience; most are too busy elsewhere to engage on Twitter with what I share. So I adjusted my tweets to release across all time zones every day except Saturday, and now I get much better results. Audiences vary, so you'll have to do your own testing, but you can see how important it is to make it a part of your sharing strategy.

When something resonates, that means people are listening—and you should take advantage of that window of time for further engagement. However, keep in mind that the window is likely to be short and attention will wane over time, so frequency is another thing to test.

Knowing When Not to Share

There are also a lot of timing challenges in how much you talk about yourself versus talking about other things. Even if you have good news to share every day about your company, that doesn't mean you should. Good news (as well as bad news) should be well timed. Jumping all over something the minute you find out about it may have negative consequences or reduce the impact of what you're sharing down the road. For instance, when I started writing this book, I didn't share the title or subject right away. It's a good thing I didn't, because later, when I received the opportunity to deliver my

TED talk, they required that it be about a subject I had not publicly shared. While there is no way to know that these opportunities are on the horizon, I've seen that waiting just a bit before releasing big news can result in better timing karma. Also, when a company or an individual constantly shares good news about themselves it can start to sound more like noise than news.

The TMI Factor: When Does Sharing Become Too Much?

Closely related to knowing *when* not to share information is knowing *what* not to share, or the "Too Much Information" (TMI) factor. We have all seen personal Facebook profiles where an individual shares every moment of their lives, from their first bathroom break to what they're planning for dinner and everything in between. TMI, right? Whether you're sharing for personal or business reasons there's a balance to achieve between sharing style and frequency. Weighing the threshold of posts for each channel with the *type of content that will most likely resonate with your audience* will help you limit the TMI factor that turns off audiences. A funny (but true) quote by Tucker Carlson sums it up: "Unless you know a lot more about something than I do, I'm not really that interested. I have too much information already."

The Blurred Lines between Automation and Human Interaction

One of the top questions I consistently get asked is, "How do I scale my engagement across social?" Managing large social communities, or listening all the time, really is time consuming, and we've developed all kinds of time-saving apps and software to help us automate the process. And herein lies the distinction: processes can be automated; one-on-one conversations meant to relationship-build cannot. The bottom line is that meaningful, one-on-one conversation requires human-to-human interaction and a personal touch. It's the blending of the two that's an art form—and it's always evolving.

When you can automate, in the right places, the human touchpoints within any campaign, product release, or general sharing system, you've hit the jackpot. To achieve this, we use the rule of thirds split between automation, sharing, and one-on-one interaction (which is how we approach it at PureMatter, and how I approach it for my individual brand).

Word of caution: while great tools help us automate the process, too much automation of engagement gets us into trouble. The more complex we get with our automation systems, the harder we have to work at humanizing what we do. Unfortunately, the science of automation has taught your target audiences to distrust most marketing. For instance, when you're doing email triage every morning do you question whether a particular email is from a real person or if it's an email blast that's been personalized? Are you suspicious that the ads you see are retargeted? Do you stop looking at your direct messages on Twitter because all you seem to receive are automated messages? Your audience is just as sick of being bombarded with automation as you are.

In this discussion of automation, let's also consider the human error factor. Currently, there is no automated system that prevents humans from making mistakes or social gaffes online. As companies, we've been used to having a little space between developing content and distributing it, but digital sharing, especially the immediacy of social, has made many of us wish there were more filters in place to prevent human mistakes from seeping in.

But where should we draw that line? People want us to be more human online, but part of the discomfort many companies have with embracing social business is the possibility of embarrassment due to human error. Some of the gaffes committed online by corporations have been more than just embarrassing—they've been career ending. However, companies are learning to demonstrate humanity, rather than knee-jerk reactions to save face. That's a good thing.

In the corporate world, though, there's still a little too much emphasis on appearing perfect. People are surprisingly forgiving of brands when they own up to mistakes. Unfortunately, some haters out there love to point fingers and jump all over imperfections; but for the most part people understand that mistakes happen.

Sometimes, however, the tools we use to automate some of our content distribution and sharing processes can exacerbate a mistake. There are times when you need to turn off automation altogether and just react as a person. Depending on the level of severity, when something is blowing up online that you need to deal with that's generally not a good time for automating Twitter, emails, or other platforms—especially if you have a complex mix. How do you know that your creative for any one platform isn't referencing an already negative controversy? The safest course of action is to shut off automation immediately; the second safest is to audit immediately and take action where necessary.

Just as companies plan for a public relations crisis, they must also take precautions to minimize damage from a social sharing crisis. Heed the following:

Prepare a social crisis-management plan: A mistake is made or something bad happens, and suddenly it goes viral. What do you do? Crisis management is probably the scariest thing companies face online today, and success is definitely tied to timing but also to demonstrating your humanity.

This is where having a social crisis-management plan in place is essential. The best plans involve getting all departments together and brainstorming every possible negative scenario regarding product or service (from minor issues to worst-case-scenarios), then developing a written plan for responding to those issues, including which department should respond, what can be said, and when. Many companies have found out the hard way just how quickly a bad experience can spread on social channels. It's how and when you react to it that makes the difference. Rather than delaying your response while you figure out what to do, or giving a kneejerk reaction that points blame rather than fixes the problem, a well-thought-out crisis management plan allows faster response time before an issue gets a chance to go viral or a foot-in-mouth response causes bigger damage.

Here's a great example of this: US Airways brilliantly responded in a very human way after an employee accidentally tweeted an incredibly graphic NSFW (not suitable for work) image while trying to resolve a customer complaint. The Twitterverse went wild and bludgeoned the brand with jokes, parodies, and the typical "somebody's getting fired" schadenfreude that often happens when a big brand fails publicly on social channels. US Airways quickly deleted the tweet and apologized, but even better, they didn't scapegoat their employee, backpedal, or try to whitewash the problem. "The individual who was involved will not be reprimanded or anything of the sort," said spokesman Matt Miller. "It was an honest mistake." The airline's timely and empathetic response was refreshing and showed an unprecedented willingness to be human in reaction to the crisis. I hope more brands follow suit.

Another example of a brand that gets crisis response right is Airbnb, which learned from a previous incident just how important stepping up can be. In March 2014, crisis management blog authors Jonathan and Eric Bernstein reported[18] how quick action on the part of the brand (including prior planning and great crisis communications) saved the day for one of its hosts. I can't even imagine how Ari Teman of Manhattan must have felt when he found out the Airbnb guests who booked his apartment for a wedding opened it to a public orgy that was advertised via social media! Thankfully, Airbnb's response was swift and helpful. According to the article, within twenty-four hours the travel

---

18   http://managementhelp.org/blogs/crisis-management/2014/03/29/an-orgy-in-your-apartment-airbnbs-crisis-management-win/

brand sent a locksmith to change Teman's locks, put him up in a hotel for a week, and wired him $23,817. Then they immediately issued a strong statement to media outlets (which had already posted stories on the incident) that reflected the brand's humanity and responsibility. Many either circulated it verbatim or used it to update their original articles. This is a perfect example of how crucial it is to be timely in responding to a crisis.

Can we prevent any and all mistakes on social channels? Of course not. But we can all act more human about the mistakes we make. We're all going to fail. The point is to embrace those failures and learn from them. So many people expect companies to fire employees that have made mistakes on social media because so many companies have been doing just that—and that's sad. Yes, responding to emergency situations needs to be timely, and having a crisis management plan is essential, but our actions should also reflect our human side. Haters are going to hate, but if we're courageous enough to act with empathy, understanding, and forgiveness in our communications, we will have a much better chance of winning the hearts and minds of our audiences.

Develop a plan that takes these types of things into consideration. Plan for every possible negative thing that could be said about your brand and how you would react socially so you're not scrambling to quell a hatefest in the middle of the crisis. Most importantly, be prepared with statements for the crisis scenarios you developed in your plan. What you say and when you say it matters a great deal; if you don't get those two things right, your entire plan will fail no matter what.

Create a social governance policy: Decide who is going to do what and when. This is critical for every business, but especially for larger companies. There's no way one person can take down an enterprise-level amount of sharing during a crisis. Break it up into manageable chunks across digital and traditional, and assign people to the process, making sure they understand their respective roles.

Vet turnoff switches on your social technologies: When you're researching sharing technologies, ask these questions: Is there a switch? How do I turn this off in a hurry? Ask vendors about their procedures and make sure they align with yours before you jump in. In fact, asking about their procedures is one of the first things you should do before investing in these technologies.

I'll illustrate this with something that happened to me during the Boston Marathon bombing. While waiting to board a two-hour flight, I queued up fifteen or twenty posts from Triberr (a blog amplification network founded by my friend Dino Dogan) as part of my sharing strategy on Twitter. The tweets were buffered to release the rest of the day. Unfortunately, the bombing happened while I was in flight, and I had no way to turn off the Triberr shares from the air. The fact that I was tweeting during the crisis incensed some people (and not just about my tweets, but anyone who tweeted during the tragedy), and it quickly blew up into a social brawl with a few haters that lasted twenty-four hours.

Whether you're automating certain processes or someone just posts something by mistake, committing a social gaffe like this is a very human problem and something every brand should be aware of and think through when planning their sharing strategy.

Practice with fire drills: Don't wait for a crisis to happen before practicing an automation shutdown (or any aspect of your crisis plan). Practice regularly so everyone knows what it feels like to get everything done.

Will social technology support filters that help people prevent gaffes online? Right now Twitter doesn't have a filter to say, "Are you sure you want to post this?" But they should. Humans are humans, and we all make mistakes. Eventually more safeguards will be developed, but that's not to say we can design foolproof safety nets online so no one ever makes a mistake. That's just not possible, and we shouldn't even expect it. What we should expect is to deal with mistakes appropriately, as well as transparently, owning up to them and taking care of them in a timely manner. Let's stop taking ourselves so seriously!

Scheduling as a practice: Lots of tools can help us time what we share online, but I want to make a distinction here: it's okay to schedule content sharing, but it's not okay to schedule engagement. There's a big difference.

Scheduling tools like Hootsuite and Buffer App can be particularly useful as your social audience grows. Both are extremely popular because they have an auto-scheduler feature that takes into account the activity of your particular audience. You can schedule your social updates to fall at the best times because the software runs analytics on the times your followers are most engaged and actively sharing. No assembly required on your part.

However, listening is another good way to use a scheduling platform like Hootsuite, especially if you pair it with your CRM system to give your team a 360-degree view of your sales pipeline. Some CRM systems like Nimble can help organize your social contacts into lists and tag conversations to track across platforms. This comes in especially handy as your social connections grow. Keeping track of thousands of conversations and nurturing relationships across platforms can quickly become overwhelming without good tools and a team approach.

At PureMatter we use Hootsuite search streams to identify high-value prospects and Twitter lists. As we filter through social contacts and conversations, contact information is sent from Hootsuite to Nimble, where it is tagged to organize it into leads, prospects, or customers. What happens next is up to the human team members.

You can't automate human interaction, but combining these two tools helps us find many more sales opportunities (which can often start with just a tweet or another social signal) and track and nurture them. Hootsuite allows us to turn social media conversations into meaningful relationships, while Nimble tracks and reports on all business opportunities so we close more deals in less time. Pairing these two platforms allows us to be more responsive to people, which has increased sales while decreasing spending on time and resources.

Time your responses: Responding to people in a timely manner is every bit as important as listening; it's one of those things that can differentiate you in the marketplace. However, the amount of social conversation happening on a daily basis can be enormous. So many brands get overwhelmed by this that they don't pay as much attention to timely response as they should. Too often they sit in fear and just push content, staying silent in response to the thousands of loyal fans who engage. You might be asking yourself these questions: How can I possibly respond to everyone? What if the conversation gains so much momentum that it creates more than we can handle? How do I say the right thing each and every time so I don't get into trouble?

Responsiveness is tied to the science of listening, so if your listening systems are in place, you don't have to fear that something will fall through the cracks. Getting your timing right isn't hard, just a matter of educating your team on proper responses and setting expectations for timeliness. Now, while all your responses online should be timely, there are three basic categories of responsiveness; they all come down to responding as you normally would in real-life situations as a polite, thoughtful human being.

Someone shares or asks a question about your content: When people respond to something you've shared online, you and/or your team should be paying enough attention to like their comments, thank them by name, answer their question, etc. You would show your attentiveness the same way offline, wouldn't you? So be nice. Be thoughtful. Be as human online as you are in person. Timing isn't supercritical here as long as it's within a business day (or whatever fits the scenario).

Customer service response: Here again, how do you handle customer service issues when someone picks up the phone and calls you? I'll bet you're on top of them, because you know this directly affects your bottom line. If improving customer service by building a social presence and being responsive is your goal, that's great! Keep in mind that people often resort to social contact after they've tried traditional means, unsuccessfully, to solve a problem (à la Courtney and our Naked Wines experience). They might already be angry or frustrated, so listening for and responding immediately (or as closely as possible) to those customer service issues is paramount. When someone builds up the courage to tweet a brand and broadcast their unique experience (either as a thank you or negative feedback), the worst thing they could receive is radio silence. Just like in real life, when people want to talk with a brand and it falls on deaf and mute ears, the perception is that they don't care and negative sentiment spreads. Everyone wants to be heard and acknowledged, and no one wants to feel as if your response is an afterthought. By responding in a timely, relevant way, you can see connections start to scale, and fans will move toward you because you demonstrated that you care. It also opens opportunities to delight people and move them from fans to raving fans.

The trick is to scale this exercise as more consumers turn to Twitter as a customer service resolution channel. This underscores the importance of training those with direct contact to your customers; that's the most valuable interaction a brand can have with their customers, and whoever is interacting with them had better be prepared with a response strategy and governance plan.

Planning for real-time: Responding as much as possible in real time is even more important than being timely. This is what truly differentiates a company and makes them the envy of the marketing world. How can you set your team up for real-time success? First, you need to know there's a difference between being real-time and last-minute.

Companies have found a way to jumpstart social sharing around their brands by growth hacking, or taking advantage of a trending topic with a unique and memorable message that points back to their own brand. To be the first to piggyback on a trend or topic requires judicious listening, but it can pay off in spades.

Okay, this wouldn't be a section on real-time social marketing if I didn't mention Oreo's "You can still dunk in the dark" tweet from the 2013 Super Bowl. Recently, I sat down at SXSW in Austin with Bonin Bough, vice president of global media and consumer engagement at Mondelēz International, Oreo's holding company, to chat about their now infamous event. Although that one social moment gained worldwide attention, he actually saw it as a failure, he said. "For as much attention as Oreo got for being quick with our 'Dunk in the dark' tweet, we just left it there. In hindsight, we should have created a campaign around that moment that so many people connected with it. If we had developed a microsite and creative to keep that momentum going for several months, imagine how much more we would have gotten out of that experience. Instead, we just moved on, and that won't happen again," Bough explained.

Most companies need to plan now for something that will happen months from now. The largest unexpected real-time moments are the ones that are well planned using listening as a strategy to drive responses (and ultimately ongoing conversations and campaigns) that will resonate. This takes a quick-witted team as well, but planning ahead helps you to TITS—to "Think It Through, Seriously."

This strategy works equally well for product launches, events—even crisis management—but planning your real-time response style with your team ahead of schedule is crucial. It allows everyone to be on board with creative juices flowing so your responses are not only genuine, but so that they can be plugged into your sharing engine to run like clockwork.

Listening for ways to delight your customers with something unexpected is another positive way to use real-time social marketing. A good example is Citi Bike NYC, which helped one of its customers, Paull Young (director of digital media at charity: water), when he tweeted that he fell off his Citi Bike on the way to a meeting and ruined his pants. Partnering with J. Crew, the fast-thinking social team at Citi surprised Paull immediately with a "Help is on the way!" tweet and a gift card for a new pair of jeans he could pick up on his way home. In fact, the card was waiting for him after he got out of his meeting.

Not everyone can marshal the resources of a big brand like Citi or J. Crew to ride the wave of a popular trend. However, even the smallest company can use the science of listening and timing to make memorable moments with their audiences, and these kinds of experiences are like "Kodak Moments" (remember that great slogan?), which I equate with shareable moments because they strike an emotional chord. Creating Kodak Moments means more than just riding the wave of what's popular and putting it out there at the opportune time. It means always listening for opportunities to connect, build relationships, and deliver value.

A Kodak Moment I remember with delight: IBM tweeting me a special Valentine's Day social card. It was part of a thank-you to their influencers, and each one was crafted individually, which meant a lot to me.

Michela Stribling, program director of social business for IBM, said I wasn't the only person who felt this way. The Valentine's Day campaign, she said, was a simple, sweet way to share a little digital love. "We literally wanted to show people how much we appreciate everything that they do for us— from retweeting our content to commenting on our blogs to attending our conferences," said Michela. "It was an act of digital kindness with no expectation of anything in return, and the irony is that our community responded with unbridled enthusiasm."

Every business can (and should) seek ways to create these kinds of moments for their customers, partners, and influencers who make up their social community. Whether you plan them ahead or develop them spontaneously in real time, if the effort is genuinely human, the result will always be positive.

A good overall sharing strategy is always a blend of planning, finding the right tools, and practicing authentic human engagement. Yes, timing is critical—both saving time and being timely with what and when we share. However, the important thing to remember is that automation should always be tempered by keeping the end goal in mind: building human relationships. Relationships are what move us forward individually and as brands. But which type of relationships are responsible for the most growth? Hands down, they are the ones you build with influencers—your personal and business advocates. Identify and nurture those relationships with sharing, and you can grow your business at scale.

CHAPTER 7

REDEFINING INFLUENCERS INSIDE AND OUT

n today's world, what exactly is influence? The Oxford Dictionary defines it as the capacity to have an effect on someone's beliefs or actions. So who are today's influencers? It used to be that people of influence were considered movers and shakers with celebrity status: a sports figure, an actor, a politician—someone with a huge audience and a media platform. But these people don't hold the same sway in our lives as they did over a decade ago. The old celebrity influencers had what I call "paid fake credibility." We doubt sports figures actually wore those shoes or that a paid celebrity really uses that skin tonic to make their lives better. Now we're no longer looking at TV commercials—we're asking friends on social what they think.

In fact, social has changed the dynamics of influence and leveled the playing field. Now everyone can be an influencer. If you can share something socially, you have the power to influence people. We do it every day when we share things, whether it's in a face-to-face conversation or a digital one. Our friends and family (even strangers who share Yelp reviews) have more power to influence our buying decisions than any TV celebrity or guru. It all comes down to trust. Who do you trust more?

Here's a perfect example of this: when I needed a new garage door, I called a company that I'd found online for a quote. When a rep showed up for a look, he told me it would cost a thousand dollars, but he couldn't tell me how that broke down in terms of time and resources. In fact, he said he'd have to call his manager to find out. What?!? Even when I pressed him he couldn't tell me how he came up with that figure. Not much trust there. Plus, he charged me forty dollars just to give me the quote!

I did more digging next and found some local companies, one of which had 450 positive Yelp reviews (and not a single negative one). Even though I don't often search Yelp reviews, that number made me take a closer look. I Googled the company and found that it was linked to a couple of my friends who had said good things about them, and I also looked at a neighborhood site that showed several of my neighbors had used the contractor and left even more good reviews. Better and better.

Ultimately I contacted them, and I had an excellent experience with this company. The technician came out within twenty-four hours, showed me pamphlets and brochures, gave me all kinds of options and pricing, and promised to install the door for about half the price that the first guy quoted. I could see why they had over 450 positive reviews!

Just think, ten years ago this kind of information sharing just wasn't possible. If you wanted to check out a contractor you had to rely on your immediate family's or friends' referrals. Today's social proof opportunities with review sites and recommendations illustrate the power communities (and the individuals in them) have on our personal and business lives.

Social proof isn't the only measure of someone's influence, however. For instance, I'm thinking of buying a bike, and the person I'm going to go to for information isn't the sales guy at the store (whose sole interest is selling me something). I'll go to my friend Dave, who doesn't use social media and doesn't have a Klout or Kred score (which are only benchmarks for social anyway), and has no interest in selling me a bike. Having spoken with him, I'm confident that he knows everything there is to know about bikes, so I trust him as an influencer on the topic. Influence is all about building trust and credibility. Dave and I share a common interest and have cultivated a friendship, so that level of trust is what will be the biggest influencer in my buying decision. But what about your customers? Whose opinions do they value?

Finding and Cultivating Influencers in Your Industry

I spoke to Ekaterina Walter, marketing innovator, author, and Sprinklr evangelist, about how to find influencers. She talked about four ways you can identify them for your industry:

Identifying Influencers

One of the most effective ways to identify influencers is through being present inside that industry. Most of the time, if you know your industry well, you know where the communication is happening. I'll give you an example: take Intel's software team. About five or six years ago, they started to plug themselves into software developing conversations in specific niche forums where developers hang out. They started seeing and understanding who the most engaged people were, but also which people really impacted and sparked the most conversation. In niche movements, it's all about sparking the conversation.

They knew their industry, identified the relevant people in that industry based on conversation, and built relationships with them. It takes time, but nurturing those relationships long-term will pay off.

The second way to identify influencers is to just go out there in the wild and say, "All right, who is mentioning our brand more often than not? Let's invite them to engage with us, or bring them into our specifically built, branded networks of influencers."

A third way is to tap into your current customers, and I'm not talking about only loyal customers. Just because a customer is loyal and comes back often doesn't mean they are your biggest advocates or they're actual influencers. If you don't try to identify whether they are, you'll be leaving a lot of low-hanging fruit behind. Tap into your CRM and look at your purchasing data, loyalty data, or loyalty program data if you're a CPG retailer, etc. Identify people that you might have overlooked that could be influencers or influencer advocates—those who have high reach, but are also passionate advocates for a particular brand or product.

Now there's a fourth way that we can also touch on, which is employee advocacy. Again, low-hanging fruit. There are lots of employees that are very connected and known in the industry that brands simply don't allow to activate.

Always Start with People

Everything starts with the people part of this, beginning with buy-in and support from top-level executives. Behavioral change has to start at the top, and organizational models have to change to allow internal collaboration and idea flow from employees and partners. We've seen too many businesses grab at the technology (or platform) piece first, totally ignoring the people that are involved in processes like creating social policies, integrating technology, and providing customer support. A good example of this is hiring an outside agency to look at your internal or customer-support processes without first picking the brains of your employees who live with those processes every day. With their deep understanding of your business and its goals, employees are like a diamond mine in your backyard. For instance, did you know that Amazon Prime membership, which accounts for close to 20 percent of the retail giant's revenue, was an idea floated by an Amazon employee?

The flipside of that coin is allowing employees to tell their own stories externally (not just re-tweet or promote company-sponsored content). We know how shareable stories are, and allowing employees to share their own stories on their own channels about your brand, product, or culture is a powerful form of advocacy. It's trusted content that you don't have to create (and it's in your back pocket!).

Once your people have their minds wrapped around your new goals of collaboration and sharing, the next step is to create workflows and other processes that enable those goals to take shape. Social media policies, technology integration, reworking customer support and crisis management to fit—all of these processes need to be brainstormed and laid out with everyone's input. For instance, who's going to be responsible for monitoring and listening on each channel? What will your content workflow look like? What are your benchmarks for measurement?

Most importantly, identifying and selecting the tools you'll use to monitor online conversations, collaborate internally, and manage customer relationships should always come after your people and process goals are worked out. Trying to adapt your people and processes to a set functionality can be like trying to get a sports team across the country on bicycles. The solutions need to fit your people and end goals—not the other way around.

True Influence Is #H2H: The Leadtail and PureMatter "Influencers That Drive Social Media for the Brands We Love" Report

On the heels of my book *Human to Human*, we decided to embark on a different type of influence research project.

To transcend the world of lists and rankings, we partnered with Leadtail to define new engagement styles that tell us more about the humans behind the influence in social marketing.

I found this project rewarding because it demonstrated the ability to go beyond the superficial rank and file of typical lists. We wanted to go deeper than the obvious data most lists use in their creation because part of being human means working your ass off to make something complex look easy.

Carter Hostelley, CEO of Leadtail, explains the premise:

> There's no question that technology has made it easier than ever to analyze, segment, and target buyers. Yet marketers still struggle to develop compelling brand content and effectively engage on social media. Why is that? Because we forget that it starts with thinking of our customers and prospects as people. Not database segments, email addresses, or users ... but real people.

Our chosen group of the Top 30 influencers were people who work daily on strategy and execution for their brands. The executives we looked at for our study were a mix of rising social media stars and digital veterans, all of whom wield influence over the strategy and execution of social and digital brand communications. These influencers are highly sought after by brands and vendors that sell to marketing decision makers—whether they're pitching marketing tech, event sponsorships, ad space, or airline tickets.

We analyzed individual Twitter handles (versus brand handles), because like many people, these influencers use Twitter to engage friends, colleagues, brands, and media on behalf of themselves *and* their brand. Unlike survey data, we wanted to summarize behavioral data—what the executives we studied empirically DO: who they mention, what they share, and how they engage.

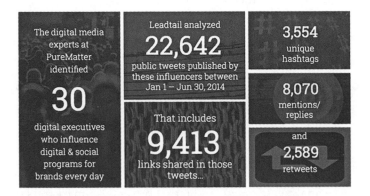

After we analyzed the Twitter behavior of our thirty influencers, three engagement styles emerged, each with its own unique characteristics:

- **Conversationalists:** most likely to mention others; focused on engagement
- **Amplifiers:** most likely to share links and retweets; focused on topics
- **Brand Champions:** most likely to share multimedia; focused on brand

Conversationalists

Conversationalists are interested in dialogue and engagement. They're the ones who bring new voices into conversations and bridge the online/offline gap by building authentic relationships in both areas. We defined conversationalists as people who had a "mention to tweet" ratio > 0.95, which means almost every tweet they publish mentions someone. Conversationalists regularly share links, but at a rate somewhat lower than the amplifiers.

You're a conversationalist if you have a lot of conversations online. You ask questions, make comments, and find areas of common interest with the people you engage on social media. When you share content, you add your own perspective or ask others for theirs.

How can you reach and engage other conversationalists? By definition, these are people who want to engage, so reach out to them with genuine questions or comments. Conversationalists are natural engagers and typically forge deep relationships with their connections, especially if they meet face to face.

Amplifiers

Amplifiers act as our trusted curators. They know their business top to bottom, left to right, and have put in the time to build up trust, credibility, and an audience around their areas of expertise. Amplifiers make sure the best ideas are shared and heard on social media.

You're an amplifier if you're someone who shares links and/or if you retweet others' content at a higher rate than conversationalists or brand champions.

You're an amplifier if you tend to center around one or two core themes, sharing content and perspectives that build your personal brand around those topics. You are an effective amplifier when you hone your listening skills and pick out unique POVs and information from the sea of "me too" content. This is how you build trust with your audience and become a sought-after influencer for others that wish to reach your same audience.

You're part of a discerning bunch, not particularly likely to share others' content simply because they ask (or pay!). Only when someone brings something to the table that enhances your credibility in your area of expertise or expands your audience will you be inclined to share.

Brand Champions

Brand champions are powerful advocates for their brand and important signatures of authenticity. After all, if the people responsible for creating the brand don't reflect the core values and lifestyle the brand promises, all the marketing in the world won't help!

You're a brand champion if your tone and content are consistently in strong alignment with your brand's values and message.

Brand champions are the most likely to cross-post from multiple networks through Twitter and to share more types of content, e.g. location check-ins, photos, and videos.

In large part, brand champions are multimedia mavens—you show, don't tell. You demonstrate the value of what you have to say in a way that shows you "get" who you are in alignment with your brand.

Who Are They?

You can see how our influencers were categorized in the complete Leadtail report, but here's a full list of those we named. Follow, then engage with them, and watch how they work; they all are worth emulating, and I am sure they would appreciate a shout-out!

Empowering Employees to Be Influencers

When it comes to employee advocacy, company leaders often ask the wrong question about word of mouth and social: How do I get my employees to share my information? The question they should be asking is, "How can I help them share their own information?" Most people want to help but will only be inspired when they feel their company shares a vested interest in them. Your employees can

Susan Beebe
Tyson Foods
pg. 24

Abigail Cusick
BravoTV
pg. 38

Karen Lee
Stanford Business
pg. 16

Padmasree Warrior
Cisco
pg. 21

Pete Blackshaw
Nestle
pg. 25

Frank Eliason
CITI
pg. 12

Josh Martin
Arby's
pg. 17

Caroline Watson
H&M
pg. 42

Andrew Bowins
MasterCard
pg. 26

Jeanette Gibson
HootSuite
pg. 13

Erich Marx
Nissan N.A.
pg. 31

Farryn Weiner
Michael Kors
pg. 43

LaSandra Brill
Symantec
pg. 27

Dan Gingiss
Discover Fin. Svcs
pg. 29

Chad Parizman
Scripps Networks
pg. 40

Lisa Weser
Anheuser-Busch
pg. 44

Don Bulmer
Shell
pg. 28

Lorena Hathaway
Pitney Bowes
pg. 14

Maria Poveromo
Adobe
pg. 18

Kaitlyn Wilkins
Burberry
pg. 32

Tami Cannizzaro
IBM
pg. 11

Kevin Hunt
General Mills
pg. 30

Julia Quinn
Amtrak
pg. 19

Todd Wilms
SAP
pg. 33

Jamie Coomber
Converse
pg. 36

Eliot Johnson
KPMG
pg. 15

Marty St. George
JetBlue
pg. 41

Jay Cooney
OMNI Hotels
pg. 37

Bill Johnston
Autodesk
pg. 39

Micheala Stribling
IBM
pg. 20

be your best advocates; they care about your brand and want to share their experiences, but need guardrails to be sure they're safe, so setting up sharing guidelines and making it easy for them to share safely is critical.

Here's a very important operational element of that: If you're going to ask members of your team to be influencers and thought leaders, and you want them to convey information that's of interest to customers and prospective customers and business partners, you need to give them the time and resources to do that. Asking them to spend a significant amount of their time creating content and being a thought leader in addition to what they're already doing is neither fair nor effective. You've got to be thinking about the other responsibilities on their plates. Thought leadership isn't something that can be switched on and off or Swiss cheesed around other activities. To be effective influencers, employees can't be thinking, "Thursdays from ten to 10:07 I'm going to be a thought leader, but then I have to go to the next meeting," yet that's what a lot of people are faced with in corporate situations. They don't know when they're going to have time to pull this off.

Another aspect of empowering employees is empowering the *right* employees. Not everyone has the aptitude for being a thought leader, and picking the wrong people just isn't going to work. No matter how much you show them how to share your content or try to cajole them or motivate them, it just never seems to happen.

In a guest post on my blog called "Find Thirstier Horses," Mark Waxman, the CMO of CBIZ, says that the right employee advocates sometimes come from surprising places:

> Sometimes you really can lead a horse to water, but can't make them drink. Fortunately, the solution is simple: Find thirstier horses. Yes, they are out there. They may not be the ones you first think of. They are often not your managers, perhaps not your leaders. They may not be the first ones that came to mind. But buried in the cubicles and backrooms of every company are the young, socially aware and active employees looking for an opportunity to grow their career... using a path that they are uniquely qualified to follow! Find thirsty horses, encourage and reward them, and you are likely to find a surprising phenomenon: all those other horses that you previously led to water but couldn't make drink? Guess what? They are going to start getting mighty thirsty.

In thought leadership, the collective social voice of an organization's employees can often be more credible and powerful than the voice of the organization itself. Finding and empowering your most passionate and social media savvy employees (as well as giving them the tools and the time to be true thought leaders) can help you build an enthusiastic internal army of advocates.

One such tool is Dynamic Signal, an employee advocacy platform that is making big strides with clients like SAP, General Mills, and Allstate, but the proof is in the pudding. One of their tech clients saw firsthand how effective their advocacy platform, VoiceStorm, could be. Monitoring impressions from sharing just three pieces of content (an event announcement, an infographic and a promotional offer), the company saw a 151 percent greater social reach when the content was shared by employee advocates versus official brand channels (view an infographic on the Dynamic Signal results here: http://dynamicsignal.com/2014/05/21/high-tech-industry-excels-employee-advocacy-part-one/).

Seeking Influencers

Outside of developing employee advocates, once you find influencers in your industry, how do you establish relationships with them? Influencer marketing is one method to achieve this. If you have a live event, such as a conference or trade show pertaining to their topic of expertise, a powerful way to cultivate them is to invite them as a VIP to the event. At PureMatter we worked with Cisco and IBM to develop influencer programs, with great results. For example, for Cisco Live we identified and invited twenty-two technology influencers (customers and partners with a keen interest in tech and a broad reach on social networks) to be part of the company's Cisco Champions network. Content was shared and informational briefings provided to Champions prior, during, and post-conference. This sharing activity not only helped Cisco forge deeper relationships with their advocates, but it also motivated them to create their own content (blogs, etc.) and amplify their messages. For Cisco, to create a sense of community we provided a private Facebook group to share previews of activities. We didn't ask them to blog or tweet, but provided them with tools and assets to make it easy to share their experiences, and it worked like magic. In fact, there were nine million impressions from Twitter posts within a few hours of the first keynote, and twenty-four million impressions by the third day of the four-day event.

According to Joel Comm, one of the influencers who blogged about his experience, those figures rose exponentially as the event unfolded. "The Cisco Live social media team tracked over 286,000,000 impressions of tweets created by those who used a hashtag from the event," writes Joel in his blog. "The influencer community of 20 was responsible for over 30,000,000 of those impressions! So essentially, twenty people made up more than 10% of the impressions in an audience of over 27,000 people. And that's just counting tweets, not Facebook, Google Plus, Instagram or other social networks."

Even better, numerous blog posts and articles were generated by members of the group during and after the conference. They felt valued and were excited to talk about what they experienced, extending Cisco Live's reach and impact well after the conference. Brian Moran, Small Business Marketing consultant and writer for American Express OPEN was also one of our influencers for Cisco Live. "For me, the influencer marketing program helped create bonds that I'm sure will continue to bear fruit long term. Getting to spend time with a small handful of people I already admired, along with the insider access we were given to learn the inner workings of Cisco, made me feel connected at a whole new level."

Another way Cisco practices influencer engagement is with #CiscoChampions Radio, pairing influencers with subject matter experts from across Cisco and recording their conversations for a radio podcast. These conversations range from engaging discussions about Cisco products and solutions to broader discussions about general IT trends and topics. Cisco Champions share these podcasts across their networks, resulting in increased awareness for Cisco solutions and a Twitter reach of @500K+ per month.

In addition to using live events, systems like TapInfluence can help you identify and manage your influencers so you can publish content, measure effectiveness, and share concrete results with executives on your influencer marketing efforts. Technologies like these will continue to help brands (and influencers) develop mutually beneficial relationships based on sharing. Sam Fiorella, author of the book *Influence Marketing*, says that rather than focusing on how much is being shared or how far it's being shared, technology is allowing us to analyze social conversations in such a way that we can focus on the context (or the result) of what's being shared, so influence marketing will continue to grow in relevancy.

Now that we've looked at the kinds of people who make up our influencer network and have touched on some ways you can leverage the power of that network, let's examine some of the social platforms people use to share. Granted, new ones are cropping up even as I'm writing this, but I talked to experts on the more established platforms to analyze the power of each one and what people like about using them.

CHAPTER 8

CONNECTIONS AND CONVERSATIONS: ANALYZING SOCIAL PLATFORMS

T here's something about connecting with others, sharing stories, laughs, and great conversation that feeds the soul, and that's why so many of us are drawn to social media. In essence, social is the ultimate online cocktail party. It mirrors our real-life encounters, but without the distance and physical limitations that can erect barriers to human connection. We can decide whether we want to be active in the ongoing conversation or just watch and listen and sip a beverage (without worrying about slopping a drink on someone's shoes).

Social platforms allow us to converse with people who live within a twenty-mile radius from us or network with peers across the globe in another time zone. In some ways social is even better than a physical cocktail party; we can connect with more people than we could in person, and the conversations we have there can help nurture relationships established in person by reminding us of our shared experiences in the physical world.

However, there's a sense of anonymity that can get in the way of online communication. It's really true that the eyes are the windows to the soul, and when we can't see each other in a conversation, we can't pick up on those visual body language cues that are so important in physical encounters. So how do we keep that personal connection real?

My friend Ted Rubin says that to get around the anonymity of social media we need to look people in the eye digitally, which means using digital tools and commonsense manners to reach an emotional rapport with whoever you're speaking to. Every platform has its own rules of engagement, but across the board some general rules apply—and they all involve being more human when interacting.

Here are my top five social cocktail party rules:

1. **Don't just introduce yourself and walk away.** In any networking situation (either in-person or online), there are pretty much two types of people. The ones who are there to shake as many hands as possible (the card hunters), and those that are there to have a meaningful dialogue with a handful of new people (the conversation gatherers). Socially speaking, the meaningful conversations are what build rapport and foster relationships.

2. **Let the ice melt**. Downing your drink just leaves you with an empty glass, a cold hand, and brain freeze. In other words, a quick social conversation won't get you very far, so enjoy the process of getting to know someone. Sit back and sip that drink. Let the ice melt until it breaks. Perhaps you'll find something in common with a new connection that you might have missed moving on. In social, the bar is always open. What's your hurry?

3. **Know who will be at the party.** It's always nice to know who you might meet ahead of time so you can better prepare. One of the very best inventions in social is the hashtag. Following hashtags lets you sort your conversations by relevance, so you know who is driving the topic, who will be there, and what the buzz is well before the party. When you get involved ahead of time, you can jumpstart relationships online that, if you're lucky enough to connect in person, are that much more fulfilling. (This is critical for me before conferences and events and has personally created some of the most flourishing relationships of my life).

4. **Create party lists.** I never walk away from a great conversation without listing them somewhere so I don't forget our exchange. This is vital (especially if you're not using a social CRM) as there is no way you can track every one of those conversations without putting them in a place where you can remember to visit with them again. It's contact management for social.

5. **Be first to call.** Just like in dating, there can be that "call me" dance after you meet someone new via social. My advice? Don't wait for them to call. Visit them and let them know you're there. I promise it won't make them think you're desperate. Social is about sharing great information and letting others know when you like something they've shared with you. Maybe something great was said that you want to follow up on and ask a question about. For me, my favorite thing in the morning right after I wake up is to see that someone took the time to ask a question, send me a thought, or simply retweet something I shared. It feels good, and I try to do the same for others.

Meeting someone at a cocktail party is just the first step—it's the conversation that comes afterward where the magic happens! Whether you're looking to make meaningful connections on your own profiles or you need to inspire your team to humanize your brand online, everyone should get a refresher on social networking etiquette before joining the party.

A good example of the power of sharing to create relationships came about from a campaign that I talked about in my *H2H* book. Called "90 Days to Ellen," it was a ninety-day social media experiment my friend DJ Waldow and I conducted to land a lunch date with Ellen DeGeneres to raise money for Feeding America®. In one sense it was a failure: we never did get to have lunch with her. In fact, she never acknowledged the effort at all (which was disappointing). However, the experiment was a huge success because it created relationships with lots of other people for a common cause. It generated almost seventy million impressions across social channels, almost one hundred videos created by a community of fans, dozens of memes, and over $1,500 raised for Feeding America—all for a budget of less than a dinner for two.

The social media etiquette lesson to be learned from this: Yes, social can build relationships and we can raise money, even without developing a direct relationship with celebrities like Ellen.

Speaking of meaningful conversations, let's take a look at how sharing works best on some of the top social platforms for building business relationships.

LinkedIn

As the oldest social media network for business, LinkedIn is perhaps more widely used by business leaders than any other network. However, it has changed greatly from its beginnings as an online platform for résumés. It is now a much more dynamic content-sharing network for personal profiles and brands.

LinkedIn's power has always been creating one-on-one relationships through networking, but the expansion of its content publishing platform greatly enhances an individual's ability to garner the kind of thought leadership that expands networking capabilities.

I spoke with Neal Schaeffer, CEO of Maximize Your Social and author of several books, on using LinkedIn for business, and he agrees that LinkedIn has become the premier network for building thought leadership:

> A quality share on LinkedIn is actually using the publicity platform to create content that lives on your profile. That kind of in-depth content is probably going to get more visibility than a mere status update would. But here's the caveat: You can't do it from a company page. You need to do it from a personal profile.
>
> LinkedIn is the ultimate place to generate thought leadership among business decision makers and industry influencers, and its publishing platform helps people do that.

We also discussed the steps necessary to get connections to engage with what you share; it basically comes down to three steps (and these can apply to any platform, not just LinkedIn):

1. **Get your profile in order first:** This includes profile branding, keywords, images—all the things that create a well-rounded picture of who you are. Get that infrastructure optimized so that when people find you via a LinkedIn search they see enough to want to connect with you or follow you. That's number one.

2. **Start engaging:** Once you have your profile set up and optimized, start engaging with others right away. Read what they are saying and engage with their updates first. This is an important step in building mindshare. Before you post, go and interact with what others are sharing on their status updates and in groups.

3. **Post relevant stuff regularly:** If you've been engaging with people for a while, then when you start posting things that are relevant to them, you're more likely to get engagement back because you're already on their radar.

A tool I really like that Neal employs for sharing on LinkedIn is using his personal Twitter account as an experimental test bed for content:

Twitter is where the news breaks and where you want to post the most real-time things. Every week I'll look through my Twitter posts for what got the most click-throughs, the most mentions, and the most responses. I'll pick the top ones and then share them with my other networks. The audience on Twitter is a little different than the audience on LinkedIn, but because I keep things very professional on Twitter and I'm tweeting out similar content, I think it's pretty relevant as to what type of content seems to be more popular than others. I don't do this for everything I share on LinkedIn, but it is definitely a component.

I asked Neal how effective he thought LinkedIn advertising was, and he mentioned that while LinkedIn ads are more expensive than Facebook or Twitter, there is definitely value there.

Some of my clients have built marketing funnels purely out of LinkedIn advertising. Especially where you offer white paper or webinar—something to get people into the marketing funnel. If you're selling six-figure enterprise software packages, two dollars a lead is nothing. However, targeting is essential. Set parameters to ensure that if you're getting a click that it's going to be a high quality one. That's the beauty of social ads. If you do them right, it's not only inexpensive (relatively speaking) but they can get better results the more targeted you make them.

Outside of advertising, however, which types of businesses get the most out of their LinkedIn presence? Neal and I agree that it depends on how it's being used. Big brands like Cisco are getting ROI from sharing by establishing a robust presence via their company page and getting their employees to follow the page and spread the word. Cisco's page has helped them establish and maintain thought leadership, find relevant people for job openings, and increase mindshare overall.

For smaller businesses, advertising and sharing in LinkedIn groups tends to offer more value than company pages. Because only a small percentage of your audience sees what is shared there (like on a Facebook page), it's harder for small companies to achieve scale with a company page.

For individuals, even though LinkedIn audiences are business people, the value of the platform still lies in sharing things with your connections that resonate personally or touch the heart in some way. Being human will get you more engagement than just sharing blog posts. In the end, that's really the way it works for individuals on any social platform—sharing things that give value to your LinkedIn community members.

Facebook

In the world of social networks, Facebook, with its over one billion users and counting across the globe, is definitely the elephant in the room. Facebook's Insights tell you when your audience is online, which posts generated the most engagement, and lots of other helpful statistics. At the very least these tools can help your team plan and schedule content. But what you learn also helps you plug into why those people are on that particular platform in the first place; however, it has undoubtedly been one of the more frustrating platforms because of its endlessly changing newsfeed configuration and complex Newsfeed Ranking algorithm.

Facebook has always promoted engagers. Their algorithm gives you what it thinks is the most relevant content based on your profile, your interactions, and location. Let's break this down. If I interact with you, then I am most likely going to see you on my timeline again. And if we don't engage, we are less likely to show up in each other's feeds. There are a variety of ways to change this by creating lists, buying ads, or just making a point of engaging. Yet most people on Facebook are voyeurs, because it's just easier to be entertained without the pressure of interaction. So how is this algorithm helping or predicting who the best fans, advocates, or future interacts really are?

To gauge the effects this platform has had on how brands and individuals share, I sat down with Mari Smith for a chat. Renowned for her insights on building business relationships on social media, especially with Facebook, Mari's take on the subject is direct and no-nonsense, although she fell in love with the platform in its early days in 2007 for purely human reasons.

> When I first got involved in Facebook I had a profile on LinkedIn. I also had one on MySpace but I never really went there. Every time I did, my head would hurt. Back then, remember, it was all just animated GIFs and you name it and young kids. It was just noise—just complete garbage.
>
> I'm already a natural networker. I'm pretty gregarious; I get out and about in my local community. But I tell you there was something absolutely magical about Facebook. I pulled up facebook.com and before I even signed up for an account, I'm just staring at it, going "Wow, there's something profoundly magical about this site." I just literally fell in love with it on the spot.

I liked the white space, the shade of blue. I liked the uniformity of the profiles. I didn't have to go search for where this person's about section was; it was all uniform.

And then the primary reason, from a business standpoint, is that I found very quickly that I could interact with and develop relationships with people whom I'd long admired— people whose books I read, whose seminars I attended, whose newsletters I read, and so on. So I always say that Facebook is my first love.

Facebook may have undergone many transformations since those early days, but the one thing that stands out to Mari is its impact on human communication.

Facebook became so prevalent so fast, so widespread so fast, because of humanity's desire to be more connected and to have more unity. It's a human-to-human site that answers a universal longing to belong, to know that we matter, that we make a difference. Since Facebook has come on the scene there have been more school reunions, more family reunions, more adopted children reunited with their parents, high school sweethearts reunited—you name it. That's what really tugs at my heartstrings when it comes to Facebook. Business is almost secondary. However, I've always used it for business as well.

But what about the chief complaint by businesses that Facebook's algorithm changes hinder them from getting their messages out and force them to have to advertise? Should businesses be thinking differently about how they use Facebook?

It absolutely is a big obstacle. I think most are probably looking at it from the wrong angle. The Facebook "Like" and the "People Talking about This" (PTAT) are vanity metrics, and PTAT doesn't pay the bills. People are struggling with these metrics and complain that their reach is down, that they can't get enough people talking.

But wait a minute ... are you converting the people that are talking about you? Are you converting them into true paying customers? Are you capturing leads? Are you driving traffic to your blog? To your email list? Are you getting more people to come into your store? Let's focus there and actually service the people you are connecting with.

I think that what happened is we're still in a transition period where most small- to medium-sized businesses that have limited budgets for marketing feel like Facebook owes them because they had it for free for so long. Things were looking rosy and good, and then all of a sudden it was like Facebook pulled the rug out from underneath them. When Facebook tightened its algorithm and changed to a more "pay to play" model, businesses woke up and said, "What, you want us to pay for something we got for free before?"

Obviously, since Facebook became a public company a couple of years ago, they absolutely have a fiduciary duty to make money for their shareholders. And the number one way they do that is through ads.

In a way, it's the exact same model that Google used. If a business person thinks they can get a number one spot or a first page spot on Google without investing some kind of resources, either paying an SEO expert or taking a long time to get organic SEO, they're fooling themselves. It's the same with Facebook.

You can't expect to get consistent 50, 70 or 80 percent reach of your Facebook fans in the newsfeed without investing some money and certainly some time.

So given all these shifts in social media, how should people prepare themselves for succeeding in the sharing and/or collaboration economy? How do they create content that's going to be more shareable on Facebook or any other platform for that matter?

Mari and I agree that success will depend on how well you can create stories around your personal or business brand. Mari says the three highest shareability factors for content are things that make people either laugh, cry, or say "Aww." Those three elements, combined with relevance to the audience, will have the biggest impact on future content.

Businesses that strive to include and involve their audiences in the creative process will also win, such as Vitamin Water crowdsourcing their next flavor, or Nike crowdsourcing creative shoe ideas, or Ford putting out a car for people to test and share stories about.

When brands come out from behind their corporate structure and realize that audiences don't really connect with a logo, a building, or even the shape of a product anymore—that they want to belong and gather with others that love brands and resonate with fun stories about those brands—that's when they'll succeed.

Twitter

Of all the social platforms, Twitter is the fastest moving and the most fluid. Love it or hate it, the controversial microblogging site has changed the way people share on a massive scale, and as we discussed in Chapter 5, it has been the pivot point in changing social language. So where has it been and where is it going? I spoke to Joel Comm and Dave Taylor, coauthors of a new book on Twitter, *Twitter Power 3.0: How to*

Dominate Your Market One Tweet at a Time. It's about the role they see the platform playing now and in the future.

Bryan: What are your thoughts on where Twitter has been and where it is now?

Joel: We've seen mass adoption of Twitter due to pop culture. It has become the go-to place, especially since they developed the hashtag. While Facebook has more traffic, you're likely to see hashtags in all kinds of media, including TV, movies, newspapers, magazines, and commercials. Twitter's short usernames and hashtags make it easy for lots of channels to identify with it.

When it comes to engagement, every channel is different for every person, business, or brand, and Twitter's no exception. You get out of it what you put into it. No matter where you are on social you have to find out where your engagement is. If you enjoy using it and your followers engage with you there, you should be there. However, big brands ignore Twitter at their own peril. There's no excuse for large brands to not engage there because you have a quarter of million people there in any twenty-four-hour period.

Bryan: What are some examples of brands that have used it well—and those that haven't?

Dave: Starbucks is doing a great job on Twitter. They have a really small team now—I think three people are managing their social media presence. If you do the stats, they get mentioned some crazy number of times, like one hundred times a second, yet they manage to pick and choose between those comments and come across as a very responsive corporation. I know I've interacted with Starbucks many, many, many times on Twitter. By comparison, on other social media sites when I've referenced them, I was less likely to get engagement from them.

The big piece to take away here is that we as consumers can actually feel like we've been heard by large entities or organizations on Twitter—whether it's a large sports team, corporation, or celebrity.

My friends will post, "OMG, @SnoopDogg just retweeted me!" And it doesn't matter if it was really Snoop Dogg or someone on his staff. If you go back prior to Twitter, you never got that level of interaction from any corporation. If you look at *Mad Men* as an example of what it was like before the Internet, it was a very one-way communications channel. Twitter, more than any other medium, broke that ice. It taught us to expect that they're listening and to expect that they'll respond.

Bryan: Can you give me some examples of how sharing has changed on Twitter?

Dave: We just have more tools now that make it easier. We're embedding videos and photos because we know that visual content is so much easier to consume than words. Even though we only have 140 characters on Twitter, that visual content pops out on our stream. You've seen this across the social spectrum. The reason we have the success of Pinterest and Instagram is because visuals are so powerful. It was a really strong move for Twitter to make visuals such a linchpin of tweets going forward. That stuff is just so simple to share.

When it comes to sharing, retweeting [sharing] is actually a quicker, easier process than sharing is on Facebook. With Facebook it's a two-step process. You can share content on Twitter just by clicking the retweet button.

Twitter has also changed the vote of popularity to be a reiteration of what a person says. Rather than "me too" or "like," sharing on Twitter is like saying, "I like what you've said so much that I want to actually resay it to my communities." And this produces something rather amazing in the Internet culture: "I'm not going to take your name off of it and pretend it's my work."

Bryan: Which brands or industries aren't using it the way they should?

Dave: Rather than pick on a specific industry, I think anyone that's not using Twitter as a communication device isn't using it the way they should. There are brands across the spectrum, whether they're individuals trying to sell a book or large corporations that spend too much time tweeting "Buy our stuff!" Rather than engaging, they're still treating it as a soapbox in the middle of the square where they stand with a megaphone and shout at people. That, of course, never works. The louder they shout, the more people tune them out and don't hear what they have to say.

Companies that don't put a human face on it are also making a mistake. People like to deal with people. That's why brands shouldn't use the company logo in place of the face of their social media manager. Frank Eliason of Comcast was one of the first to get this right. When they created the @ComcastCares Twitter profile, he used his picture—not the Comcast logo—and that resonated with people.

Joel: An example of a company that could be using social media to further improve their brand is Apple. To be fair, Apple is the most valuable corporation in the history of business. However, it's remarkable how little presence they have (as a company and as individual employees) on Twitter or other social media channels.

Perhaps they have the feeling that "We don't need to do this—we can engage on our terms and on our platform." However, if that type of attitude gets entrenched in their culture, it's eventually going to backfire.

Bryan: How can brands or individuals successfully leverage Twitter?

Joel: When people understand social, they spend time "being social." It's all about engaging with people and developing relationships. Even ten years ago we couldn't accomplish this reach. Back then we could never have the number of touchpoints that we have in any given day today. We can form so many more relationships now. The fabric of our lives is much richer because in some way, whether it's a brief hello or a longer conversation, we're part of each other's lives on a daily basis. People who get it right come at it from the relationship aspect. They bring value to the conversation and share what others are doing, saying, and posting. That's where the value lies.

Bryan: What about B2B industries that continue to shun social, such as manufacturing?

Dave: I feel strongly that the differentiation between B2B and B2C is a false one. A lot of time it's a lazy industry attitude. All consumers are people and B2B targets people who are consumers of business products. They're not trying to figure out "How can I find the buyer (person) who will buy my robotic system for a factory?" Instead they just think, "What company is going to buy it?" But the individuals who make those decisions are people. Somewhere, at some point, they are engaged and online. Facebook has over a billion active users and Twitter has around 280 million active users ... odds are really good that those buyers are connected somewhere. We're just going to have to wait until some manufacturing companies begin to think out of the box and become willing to try a different approach to selling their products and services. Then all the other companies in that industry will say, "Oh, *that's* how you find those people. Okay, we can do that."

Joel: It takes someone to lead the way. As Bryan says, it's all about human to human. Every manufacturing company is made up of people who are selling to other people. Also, these industries are out there looking for customers. If you're just going out there looking for customers and not engaging with individuals, you forget that *people know other people.* The person you're talking to right now might not be your potential customer, but chances are he knows someone in his network who is.

Bryan: Sometimes it seems that true conversation has died down on Twitter and it has become more promotional. Do you think that will change?

Dave: The pendulum always swings back and forth. You have a new platform, and it's very native—the original users are really excited about it—then the marketers get hold of it. They start building tools to auto-follow people and direct message people and start gumming up the works. After a while businesses start using it to really engage, a mass adoption occurs, and the pendulum swings back the other way. People are always going to try it as a way to go door to door handing out flyers, but when they see that it doesn't work, usage swings back in the other direction. It's a cycle that never ends, and there's never going to be a place of "purity." There will always be a draw from both sides.

Bryan: What about hashtags? What are people doing right, and what are they getting wrong?

Dave: The evolution of hashtags has been one of the greatest success stories of Twitter. What's fascinating to me as a social scientist is that Twitter didn't anticipate this when they started. One of the things that marks a really powerful platform is when it takes on a life of its own beyond what its developers envisioned. Hashtags are deeply entrenched. Over 50 percent of the ads in the Super Bowl included hashtags, and that's not going to go away. We're going to see more sophisticated data mining of that information in the future.

Joel: We've seen many case studies of hashtags gone wrong, where companies make themselves vulnerable. You have to be careful and not position yourself in such a way that a Twitter troll can use that hashtag against you. Some companies haven't thought that through—the ways in which a hashtag can backfire.

Bryan: Is Twitter becoming too negative?

Dave: Twitter is a reflection of the positives and negatives in our culture, and what you see in your feed is directly related to who you follow. Smart people navigate that and use tools to keep their feeds clean. You have a choice about who to follow, and that's a wonderful thing.

Bryan: Is there a followback strategy that's best for individuals or brands?

Joel: No, because everyone's goals are different. However, I would say that if you follow thousands and thousands of people, your stream can become unmanageable.

Pinterest

Cynthia Sanchez, founder of OhSoPinteresting.com, has been using Pinterest since 2011. Before starting her business in 2012, she was a full-time radiation oncology nurse. She refers to her earlier career when she discusses using social media. On her website she states:

> As a nurse, I did my best to empathize with each patient to help them heal. It is proven that if nurses relate to their patients, the nursing process goes much more smoothly and the patient has an overall better experience.
>
> I continue this approach in my business and encourage my clients to take the same approach in their social media marketing.
>
> I really do enjoy teaching and helping people find solutions. This may come from my years of being a registered nurse or from being the mother of two sets of twins. It's probably both.

She's a self-proclaimed Pinterest addict and has spoken on the topic for numerous audiences in the United States and abroad. What's her take on Pinterest as a sharing platform?

When people get started using Pinterest, the kinds of questions they ask may run the gamut, but usually one of the first questions is, "When is the best time to pin?" In her podcast "How to Get Started on Pinterest OSP-083," Cynthia states that it can take some time on the platform to find your "sweet spot" for the perfect time to pin. "Keep in mind that Pinterest is a global service," she states. If you're finding that you get more interaction on your topic in the evening in the US, remember that during the day, "it's already evening in Europe."

As with any platform, using it for a while and gathering data will inform you of the best times for your business. "There are some tools, like Tailwind, which is an analytics and pin scheduling tool, that can tell you when your sweet spot of pinning is—when you get the most re-pins and when your account gets the most activity (what day and what time of day) and relates that back to your time zone."

To maximize your visibility on Pinterest, Cynthia encourages people to curate content from beyond the Pinterest community, using tools such as Feed.ly, Swayy.co, or Google Alerts to find content to share. Like Facebook's "Edgerank," algorithm, Pinterest introduced "Smartfeed" to filter what your followers see. "It's a balancing game," she says, "because Pinterest wants to show what's popular, but also what's new. When it was a new platform, its audience wasn't as big, so you would see the same pins over and over because they were so popular on Pinterest. Now they want to bring you new things and keep it interesting. Having fresh content from outside Pinterest helps make your account more visible and your pins and boards more visible when people search for topics or browse categories."

What are some of the "rookie mistakes" that newcomers to the platform make? One is not renaming the pictures so they're more searchable, and search is key to helping people find your content on Pinterest. Cynthia noted in her podcast that when newcomers find pictures to use in their pins, they'll often "... keep the file name from whatever source they got it from. A lot of times that's just gibberish—a bunch of letters and numbers that don't make any sense. There are tools you can use, such as the official Pinterest Bookmarklet for Chrome (which pulls in a little excerpt or metadata) that you can test." She says that the questions to ask yourself when you're testing a tool like this are, "Will that [what the tool pulls in] make sense within Pinterest? Will that communicate your message, and is it searchable?"

Speaking of search, businesses should tap their website keywords (not those that are product specific, but more generic terms) as inspiration for naming their boards. "The tags you add to your blog posts—organizing things for SEO—are things you can use for board titles," Cynthia notes.

Since mobile is pushing us to ensure that our websites are responsive, she also suggests that pinners ensure the text on their images is readable on a smartphone. In other words, don't be afraid of white space. "People are more incentivized to share your content if they can read it all," she says.

What about men on Pinterest? Isn't it primarily a women-only platform? Well, that dynamic may be changing. While the current demographic leans toward women, according to a November 2014 article on Marketingland.com, the platform doubled its number of active male users in 2014, and men make up one-third of all new sign-ups. Additionally, more men use Pinterest in the US than read *Sports Illustrated* and *GQ* magazines combined. Watch out, ladies!

Does every business need to be on Pinterest? No. If your audience isn't there, or if engaging on the platform doesn't fit your overall business goals, don't go there. However, just because it doesn't fit right now doesn't mean it won't fit later. If there's one thing we know about social platforms it's that they're constantly changing.

Instagram

For pure, unadulterated sharing, you can't get more direct than Instagram, the fast-growing mobile image sharing platform that outgrew Twitter with more than 300 million active users in 2014. According to Instagram expert Sue B. Zimmerman, the platform has gained popularity quickly for three main reasons:

1. It's simple, with less noise than other platforms. Ease of use attracts people to stay on it longer.
2. Its visual content is super-easy to absorb, especially visually pleasing content.
3. Instagram is made for mobile, with an interface that makes the user experience engaging (and addicting). ˙

Instagram's instant feedback feature provides another reason for its popularity. As soon as you post images, other users seem to be waiting in the wings; you can start seeing likes and comments within *seconds* of posting. This is much faster feedback than almost any other channel.

What I find even more interesting about Instagram, however, is how it has changed the way we view photographs. In fact, an Instagram 2015 Study[19] conducted by Iconosquare puts it perfectly in the **foreword** by their CEO, Jerome Boudot:

Since 2010, Instagram has continued to develop photography to the point that it has transformed what was once a way to archive our memories into a way to share our experiences and emotions in real time.

I couldn't agree more. And as visual capturing and editing technologies continue to evolve and are made more accessible to people, this trend will only increase. The Instagram visual platform is a global

19 Iconosquare. "Instagram 2015 Study." https://secure.iconosquare.com/ instagram2015/en?utm_campaign=Instagram%202015%20follow&utm_ medium=Blog%20Iconosquare&utm_source=Blog (accessed February 18, 2015)

enablement of sharing with unlimited possibilities. No wonder Facebook invested a billion dollars to acquire it!

More enlightening nuggets from Iconosquare's study:

- Over 30 billion photos and videos published as of March 2014
- 70 million pieces of content are posted every day
- Instagram users are active: attributing 2.6 billion likes a day
- It's a network of Millennials, with 15- to 35-year-olds representing 73 percent of users
- Brands on Instagram are well received (70 percent of users have looked for a brand there; 37 percent follow between one to five brand accounts)
- Popular industries:
  - o Fashion (80 percent)
  - o Decoration (67 percent)
  - o Culture (65 percent)
  - o Audiovisual and Cinema (63 percent)
  - o Food and Beverage (56 percent)
  - o High-Tech (53 percent)

This doesn't, however, give brands carte blanche to push content. Most users choose to follow brands and share their content because they like them, not because they produce more content. According to the study, "The more an account publishes, the more engagement tends to decrease." So more isn't necessarily better. Also, while more established brands generally tend to get better engagement, even relative newcomers can get a very good or excellent engagement rate.

As with other sharing platforms, the more engaged you are with your audience on Instagram, the better your return. Creating and posting fun or inspiring visuals is your foot in the door. Following other posters and being proactive about liking, sharing, and commenting on their content are ways that individuals and brands can find success on the platform. Using the direct message feature to expand conversation can also open doors. You never know which connection will result in something more down the road or how your visual content will inspire another individual to take action.

YouTube

According to YouTube, one hundred hours of video are uploaded to the site every month. It reaches more US adults ages eighteen to thirty-four than any cable network, and it's still growing at a phenomenal rate of millions of new subscriptions a day. When it comes to sharing content, video has unprecedented potential; Cisco estimates that online video users will reach 1.5 billion by 2016. That's double today's rate.

I spoke to video marketing expert and social branding consultant Lou Bortone about how video and our usage of it has evolved and how people and brands can use video (and YouTube as a social platform) to facilitate sharing. Lou comes from a television production background working for international media brands like Fox, NBC, and E! Entertainment Television. He's also an avid social user and a parent of teenagers, so he's seen a dramatic shift in the way people not only market with video content, but interact with it.

I watch what my teenagers do, as they are kind of on the leading edge on this. It's interesting that they don't make any kind of distinction between the screens anymore. They don't care if their entertainment comes from a TV screen or an iPad or a desktop or an iPhone; it's all seamless. And that's one of the things that people who share seem to understand and seem to do well. Video sharing isn't necessarily geared toward one particular screen. It's something that can travel easily whether it's on an iPhone or an iPad or a fifty-inch screen.

As a parent of teens myself, I found his observation compelling, especially looking back at the evolution of video content alongside social media usage and the rise of mobile technology. People still share video for the same reasons they share anything else that matters to them, but video has the power to create more visual excitement in a shorter period of time. So to me, it's no surprise that video should be a key element in everyone's marketing arsenal—and it doesn't take million-dollar budgets to make big things happen.

Lou shared a story of one of his small business clients whose economical use of video drove results during a recession.

It was during the bad time with the economy when everything was in the doldrums. My client had this high-end rental property in Costa Rica, and it was empty all of the time, so she started making videos. When we started helping her with them, she had no experience, and it was like, "Okay, where is the button on the Mac that turns the Mac on?" But in pretty short order she started doing videos about life in Costa Rica. She'd go zip lining and wear the video on her head (before GoPro cameras were all the rage). And she'd just show people the experience of going to Costa Rica and enjoying it, and of course, putting stuff in about her rental property too.

I happened to look back at a couple of her videos a few weeks ago, and one of them had seventy thousand views. That puts her in the top 2 or 3 percent of all videos because the vast majority never get more than one hundred views, and she accomplished all this on a low budget. She didn't have a fancy camera, a professional crew, or a studio.

Pretty compelling, especially given that Lou's client was a solopreneur in a down economy and not very technically proficient. I asked him to identify the main drivers of her success, and he said there were three basic keys—all of which any business can (and should) emulate.

> Three things, I think, made her videos so popular. Number one is credibility. She's not saying, "Come to Costa Rica because it's really great." She's saying the good, bad, the indifferent, and she's lived down there for twenty, twenty-five years as an expat, so she's the real deal. Here's a typical American from Southern California that gave it all up and moved to Costa Rica. That was a part of it.
>
> Number two, she zeroed in on her target market—the affluent tourist—people who wanted to travel in luxury and all of that. She was getting those people and a lot of others too, so she was getting a ton of views on her videos.
>
> The third reason, I think, was that her videos were short and compelling, and she was answering the kinds of questions that people would ask who wanted to go on vacation down there: Is it safe? Is there security? What's it like? So she had a feel for those typical, frequently asked questions and turned them into short videos. So from a search engine standpoint, that also helped her because if somebody typed into Google, "Is Costa Rica safe for vacations?" chances are her video would come up. That was the exact title of the video, so she was smart to do it that way.

But what about virality? That seems to be the brass ring that so many businesses reach for when it comes to video. Is there a secret sauce? Does advertising help?

Lou has always argued that it's hard to force viral video, that it's really more of a happy accident. But he says there are certainly things you can do to make a video more shareable and more likely to go viral.

One is brevity. The shorter the video, the easier it is to share, which is why many people seem to have success with it on Instagram. Again, he harkened back to his teenagers, who introduced him to Vine.

> When it comes to Vine videos, you might think, "What can I possibly do in six seconds?" Well, the fact of the matter is, people are doing a lot. And Vines are getting passed around a lot because they're short and so easy to digest.
>
> Another common denominator is the compelling nature of the content. It may be humorous, it may be surprising, or it may be inspirational, but it's always something a little bit out of the ordinary. Think of the big, creative viral videos like "Charlie Bit My Finger." That's so silly. It's just two babies having fun in the back car seat and the little kid bites the big kid's finger, and suddenly it goes nuts. I don't know how many views it has these days, but a lot.

What can brands derive from this? Again, it's hard to predict which videos will have a viral impact, but it's good to see what others are doing to look for patterns or characteristics. *Ad Age* does a great job of watching brand videos and charting which ones hit a home run with the number of views (take a look at their Viral Video Chart here: http://adage.com/section/the-viral-video-chart/674). Mashable now sends out "Viral Alerts" generated by the amount of Web traffic their content is receiving in real time (or close to it.) Part of the fun of virality is predicting whether something will be a hit.

However, being concerned about going viral really isn't the point. Audiences are fickle, and virality is hard to predict, much less reproduce. Producing helpful or entertaining content, optimizing your videos for search, making sure they are easily shared—those are the things that can be accomplished easily via YouTube and can be measured.

As a sharing platform and the second largest search engine, YouTube has made its mark, but that doesn't mean it has the corner on the video sharing market. Mobile technology is the biggest driver behind video creation and sharing (90 percent of video is viewed/shared on mobile devices), and mobile platforms like Instagram and Vine make it easy to share with one click or one swipe of a tablet. People always have their phones with them; according to Emarketer, 72.1 million US smartphone users watched video on their devices at least once a month in 2013,[20] and video consumption on digital devices is expected to top two hundred million in 2015.[21] This is having a big impact on retail business because mobile shoppers are three times as likely to view a video as desktop shoppers, and marketers are catching on. In fact Invodo's Video Statistics: The Marketer's Summary 2014[22] showed that 93 percent of marketers use video for marketing, and those who used it in emails cited increased click-through rates, increased time spent reading email, increased sharing, conversion rates, and ultimately dollars generated as top benefits. What's not to like?

What's in Store for the Future of These Platforms?

Just as the people and brands using these social platforms must constantly innovate and evolve to stay relevant, so must the platforms themselves. Given the nature of sales and the antipathy many social audiences have for promotional behavior on these channels, how do today's companies develop scalable models for monetizing their social efforts?

Here are some ways I envision them evolving in the near future:

---

20   eMarketer, "Long Form Video Content Rivals Short Even on Smartphones," last modified December 30, 2013 (accessed February 10, 2015) www.emarketer.com/ Article/Long-Form-Video-Content-Rivals-Short-Even-on-Smartphones/1010492
21   eMarketer, "Digital Video Viewers Keep Eyes on PCs," last modified December 17, 2014 (accessed February 10, 2015). http://www.emarketer.com/Article/ Digital-Video-Viewers-Keep-Eyes-on-PCs/1011712
22   invodo, "Video Statistics: The Marketer's Summary 2014," (accessed February 10, 2015) http://www2.invodo.com/l/12102/2014-02-25/l73kt

- **The Narrowing of APIs**—This is going to be a hot topic in the social- and open-source software systems. I've always been a proponent of open source because it has helped marketers steer toward the single dashboard we have always desired, to capture in one centralized place the numerous pieces of software we use to track data across our organizational channels. Software brands have loosened their open API reins and continue to do so, but I think in 2015/2016 some social networks and software will start to pull back. Why? Well, let's consider Facebook. They want to deliver your analytics directly to you and won't want to share that through third-party software. This allows Facebook to have complete domain to drive a single-source dashboard and to completely control the outcome and ability to market. Closing APIs may start to give brands like Facebook a competitive advantage or more ways to add revenue. Everything is cyclical.

- **Video Becomes Experiential**—This shouldn't be new to you, but the growth that will happen in video marketing will take off in ways we've never seen. Again, Facebook is planning to outperform YouTube, and I believe it will. Video gives us the most context around people, companies, and things than any other online medium. But start thinking about video as experiential. This is where 3-D glasses and video start to give us the ability to play with video and experience stories, shopping, and interactions in a new way.

- **The Explosion of S-Commerce**—New video creation and hosting programs like Wistia are offering ways to generate opt-ins for email capture and re-directs to sales pages. They are also giving brands more control of the video environment as a social sales channel. Lou supports this evolution, as he explains, "There's no 'buy' button on YouTube; there's only a buy button on your site. So if you can get that traffic back to your site, that's the best of both worlds because you control the environment and the experience with fewer distractions."

CHAPTER 9

CREATING SHARED EXPERIENCES

"A re you experienced? Have you ever been experienced?" Jimi Hendrix asks listeners in the chorus of the title track of The Jimi Hendrix Experience's classic 1967 LP, *Are You Experienced*. In today's world, more marketers will soon want to start asking their customers this same question. Why? The power of shared experiences.

What Are Shared Experiences?

A shared experience is exactly what it sounds like: seeing, hearing, or doing the same thing as someone else. Although it's a simple concept, shared experiences have a deep impact on human socialization because they enhance each person's experience.

A Yale University study showed that when two people ate a piece of chocolate, they described it as more flavorful and enjoyable than when one person was eating the chocolate and the other person was doing something else. Whether it's eating food, seeing a TV show, or rooting for a sports team, sharing an experience makes it more enjoyable.

Shared experiences aren't new; people have been telling stories and communicating shared myths for thousands of years, and as technology advances, the mediums change. We had radio, movies, and television, but today we have the easiest shared experience platform society has ever known: the Internet.

The concept of shared experiences may seem simple when you're talking about it in strictly personal terms, such as sharing a beer with a friend or snapping photos of your trip to Disney World and instantly sharing them on your smartphone. However, marketers need to do a bit more thinking about how their brands are experienced by people and what makes them want to share those experiences.

Brian Solis, digital analyst, anthropologist, and author of *What's the Future of Business: Changing the Way Businesses Create Experience*, describes this very eloquently. In a video interview with the data management community All Analytics, he notes that to make the shift to the new digital economy, marketers need to step back from what they're doing now and look at their brands in a different light. "It's hard to base where you need to go when you're stuck in yesterday," he says. "My best advice is to step back, think about what you're trying to do, where you're trying to go, and what you need to get there. Start to look at things that are a little more human: values, empathy, experiences, and emotion. And start to think about how you can bring those into what you're trying to do versus what you're doing today to bridge that gap."

Brian explains that marketers need to think in terms of their brand's Shared Experience Value:

> There is your brand promise as it exists today (what your brand means, what it stands for, how you describe it on your website, and how you sell it), and then there are the experiences that

people have and share. We can use tools like data and analytics to measure not just sentiment, but what people are feeling and what they're sharing with others. If you look at that, I bet there's a gap between what your brand promise is and what people are sharing. To me, the future of all this as a marketer is to close that gap—to be reinspired. To rethink what it means to 'be' that brand and what it means to someone else so you can start to change the experiences people have and share.

Brian is spot-on because today's speed-of-thought technologies make shared experiences more powerful than ever. This means that marketers need to shift out of "business as usual" thinking and start looking at their brand from a more human perspective.

Today's shared experiences are powerful because they can cross from the Internet into the real world, and vice versa. How does this happen? Let's take a great example from a major recent event in the United States—the Super Bowl.

Shared Experiences in Action: The Curious Case of Left Shark

While the Super Bowl is a major draw for football fans all over the country, many people tune in to watch the halftime show, which is always quite elaborate.

In 2015, pop singer Katy Perry headlined the show and at one point two dancing sharks flanked her. When the shark on the left side of the screen seemed to be flubbing the planned dance routine, the world took notice—"Left Shark" was born.

Left Shark generated a flood of discussion. What started as a shared experience by viewers of the Super Bowl halftime show quickly leaped into our collective consciousness, appearing on social networks, in blogs, and prominent publications like *The New Yorker, Rolling Stone,* and *The Washington Post.* Left Shark appeared in a television commercial for major sports network ESPN. In fact, it was recently reported that Katy Perry's lawyers sent a cease-and-desist letter to a man who was selling 3D figurines of the Left Shark character.

Left Shark is a classic example of how shared experiences grow into something huge because of a cultural phenomenon.

The big question for marketers is how can the great power of shared experiences be harnessed in a way that helps them grow their brand? There are a few key tactics.

Promoting Great Shared Experiences

No matter what industry or field your business is functioning in, here are some actionable tips to create great shared experiences:

- Target experiences that are common for everyone. Think about activities people from all backgrounds and all ages can relate to, as this helps improve each person's experience. Research suggests that extraordinary experiences aren't good for helping people relate to each other. Promote your experiences on several channels. Try using the same video or image on a multitude of social networks, in your print media and so on. This helps magnify the power of the shared experience to transcend any single medium, like our friend Left Shark. Put yourself in the customer's shoes and think about what they would want. Virgin Atlantic is a relatively small airline when compared to titans like Delta and British Airways, yet Virgin is still the number two airline in the UK and one of the most memorable. How have they done it? By placing a strong focus on customer experience, including in-flight bars, massages, and manicures, and featuring a staff that has been trained to be casual and fun. Virgin figured out what people flying on commercial airlines wanted and delivered it in spades.

There are many ways you can take part in creating shared experiences. You can help create them, share them, or take part in resharing them.

We create experiences in the physical world all the time and share them by telling others about it over the phone, sending pictures online, using our mobile phones to Skype or Facetime with someone, you name it. But when two or more people collaborate to create an experience, sharing becomes exponential. Brands can take advantage of this by cocreating content with their employees. Many companies struggle with getting their employees to share the content they develop. Instead of creating content and then handing it to employees to share, the better way is to *involve them in the process of creating that content*. When an employee helps to create something, they're proud of that work and are more likely to share it once it's published. The question then becomes "What do we want to create?" not "How will we create it?" Cocreation results in more thoughtful and invested shared experiences from some of your most powerful advocates—your employees.

Leveraging the power of your community is another way brands can cocreate content. Several online media companies come to mind that do a great job of this, including Marketing Profs, Social Media Today, and Social Media Examiner. They're all driving millions of views a month to their blogs and creating visibility for the brand and the authors. Cocreating webinars and participating in Google Hangouts are other ways that individuals and brands can turn content into experience.

One of the best ways to cocreate physical experiences, but one that is under-utilized is live events. People can have positive or negative experiences during an event, so it's important for brands to not only try their best to minimize bad experiences, but to also concentrate on helping attendees build positive experiences. Make it easy for people to create mini-Kodak Moments and share them online. It could be as simple as setting up "Instagram Stations" around the event—computers where attendees can create experiences and share them on the spot. The trick is to strategically create those opportunities and let people know, "This is what to share," and "This is how to share." Also, from the brand's perspective, you need to do a good job of listening and responding to the experiences your attendees build and share—and they need to know they're being heard.

Know Your Sharers and Why They Share

In leveraging the power of community, it also helps to understand why people are motivated to share online. In 2011 *The New York Times* Customer Insight Group conducted a study called "The Psychology of Sharing: Why do People Share Online?" It was a three-phased study that included:

1. In-person interviews with people in three major urban areas: San Francisco, Chicago, and New York
2. A one-week sharing panel
3. An online quantitative survey of 2,500 medium-to-heavy online sharers

Lots of interesting data came out of this study, including the fact that participants fell into six basic categories or "personas" of online sharers. These personas were defined not just by emotional motivations, but also the role of sharing in life, the desired presentation of self, and the value of being first to share.

In a nutshell, here's how the study authors labeled sharers, including their characteristics and how they like to share:

- **Altruists:** Helpful, reliable, thoughtful, and connected. **Share via Email.**

- **Careerists:** Valuable, intelligent, building their network. **Share through LinkedIn.**
- **Hipsters:** Cutting edge, creative, building identity, young and popular. **Less likely to email.**
- **Boomerangs:** Reactive, seeking validation, sharing empowered. **Likely to share on Twitter and Facebook.**
- **Connectors:** Creative, relaxed, thoughtful planners. **Likely to share via email or Facebook.**
- **Selectives:** Resourceful, careful, thoughtful, and informative. **Likely to share via email.**

One of the key issues that sets this study apart is how these personas were built. It included something most of us don't think about—that a person's definition of self (their personal brand) has a large influence on what they share. So in creating the experiences we've been talking about, we should also consider the relationship that sharers have with each other (not just our brands).

Considering these categories, how would you characterize your audience of influencers? Are more of them altruists or boomerangs? Understanding their personalities and methods can be of huge benefit in creating the kinds of experiences that each segment is most likely to pass along.

Hashtags

A chapter on shared experiences wouldn't be complete without a discussion on hashtags. We talked a little bit about hashtags in our earlier conversation with Joel Comm on Twitter. Twitter first began using them in 2007, but hashtags have since taken on a life of their own. The lowly symbol "#" was first used on Twitter as a way to aggregate conversation around any topic, but it is now used on a plethora of other social platforms and websites, and has bled into TV, billboards, and other print media.

At first, it just seemed to be a way to group like conversations so they could be searched, but today hashtag use has expanded to allow an audience to interact live during events, such as conferences, TV shows, and political events. It has become a way for people to share something that has meaning for them and also fits into the *New York Times* persona models of how sharers like to be perceived.

Hashtags allow users to create a unique perspective on what they're sharing, whether they're tracking a term such as #socialmedia or conveying an emotion (#mylifesucks or #tgif). They also create online communities and are great tools for monitoring the visibility of a message across multiple networks. It's how I tracked the impact of *H2H* that I referred to in the beginning of Part II of this book.

While different platforms have different rules for using hashtags, there's no one-size-fits-all code of conduct. For instance, the way they're used on Twitter is far different from the way they're used on Instagram

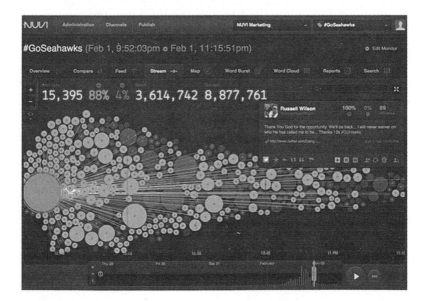

or Facebook. But from a purely sharing perspective, the hashtag gives us a unique way of gathering real intelligence about what we share, as illustrated by the following diagram from the social intelligence software company NUVI.

The bubble diagram shows you the reach of the phrase #GoSeaHawks in just over an hour during their football game with the Patriots. With such advanced data visualization technology that tracks keywords and hashtags, brands can do a much better job determining how their content is doing in real time or over a specific period. Is it resonating with people? Who's sharing it? How is it being shared?

Using hashtags is just one way we can create and track shared experiences. Who knows what's next? With all of the constant thinking up of new and innovate ways to create, cocreate, and share experiences of all kinds, we're definitely at an exciting time in our history.

New modes of sharing are allowing us to learn new things about ourselves, our audiences, and our communities. We're learning what works and what doesn't, what goes viral and what falls flat. But one thing businesses need to take away from all this is how they can incorporate sharing in an authentic and human way. How can we use sharing to serve our customers better?

CHAPTER 10

SOCIAL
~~SELLING~~ HELPING

ell me the term social selling doesn't conjure up images of a hard-hitting salesman spamming everyone in sight with promotional messaging. That said, if we struck the word "selling" from our vocabularies and replaced it with "helping," we would be much better off. We're all marketers of something, whether it's our own personal brand or a company brand. However, it's no secret that the most successful salespeople are helpers first. In fact, they're passionate about it. They listen carefully, ask the right questions, get to know their prospects as individuals, and assist them in their decision-making process. Social just gives us new and varied channels for helping, especially if you establish a good content pipeline.

For example, when I started syndicating my blog and articles on LinkedIn a couple of years ago, I began sharing that content on groups where it would add value. The former CMO of Pitney Bowes happened to be in one of my groups, liked a few of my articles, and subscribed to my newsletter. A few weeks later he sent me an Inmail on LinkedIn, noting that we had connections in common in New York, where he was based, and that he thought my content aligned with his company's needs. He expressed an interest in what my company provides and asked me to outline my services for him. Note that there was no selling here—no pitching—purely a connection sparked by content sharing. A week later his head of product marketing (based in San Jose) reached out to us. She came down and met with us about a project that turned into more business as time went on, and we later became personal friends. From those initial content touchpoints and social connections, Pitney Bowes turned out to be a major client for us, and our face-to-face connection resulted in a lasting friendship. This kind of content pipeline bears fruit for us all the time now. I don't call it selling because I've never hard-sold anyone. I've helped them, which is the best way to allow that initial connection to evolve into a sale.

This story sparked my journey into social helping; I started honing the process to improve the ways the helping resonated with people. How? By determining what content at the top of the funnel would move people to the next level and how we would use it to make it work. Since then we've constantly analyzed our content pipelines and refined our social helping process.

Although LinkedIn is a good example of a platform that's perfect for developing a social helping pipeline, it's not the only one. The trick is to unlearn hard-sell tactics and concentrate more on sharing the kind of content that sparks connection and earns trust.

Modern marketing expert and social selling evangelist Jill Rowley states that social networks are for building relationships, not pitching, and she stresses the importance of personal branding and being authentic. "Building your personal brand is the first step in social selling," she states and qualifies that by saying that sales reps "need to optimize their online presence for the buyer—not the recruiter." No one likes or trusts "quota crushers," she says. Success comes from being socially available to buyers and their sphere of influence and using educational, value-added content as currency. However, many companies are just waking up to the fact that we are no longer living in the age of the seller, but in the age of the buyer.

"There are two reasons why this is important," says Jill. "First, the data is in; reps who embrace social selling have bigger pipelines and meet their quotas more often. Second, you don't have a choice. The buying process has changed, and we can't go back. Buyers are now self-educating, using search and social networks to research and explore solutions to their problems. I don't think we've had enough awareness that the sales process is dead and long live the buying process—we're just not there yet."

Alice Myerhoff, business development sales consultant and author of the book *Social Media for Salespeople,* says salespeople improve their brand awareness and gain trust by frequently interacting on social channels with potential customers. In episode nine of my podcast series *From the Author's Point of View*, Alice, who appeared as a guest, stated, "There's the saying in marketing that someone has to interact with a brand seven or eight times before they're willing to transact. Think about that in a sales context. How many times does someone have to interact with you to feel like they can trust you and know who you are, so they're willing to transact with you?"

Alice's statement really resonated with me, because I've seen it in my own personal (and business) sharing journey. For staying top of mind, frequency and consistency of content sharing matter a great deal on social channels—and the more complicated the sale, the more important quality sharing becomes, as does aligning your brand to be in a helping position across channels.

According to a Forrester/ResearchNow report commissioned by LinkedIn,23 the more complex the purchase decisions, the more information buyers have to sort through. Trade events, blogs, vendor websites, conferences ... the sheer volume of information can be overwhelming, so more and more decision makers turn to social networks to validate this information with peers and experts. Professional social networks like LinkedIn, personal social networks, and microblogs help these buyers find relevant information quickly, give them access to a broader peer network, and provide channel(s) for connecting with vendors. So developing that pipeline and creating touchpoints at each channel are where sales teams might need some help refocusing their efforts.

When Jill Rowley trains sales teams, she teaches that the social selling process is supported by "Five Pillars":

1. **Building your personal brand:** retooling your social profiles so you show up as a thought leader, not a quota crusher.
2. **Using the ABC principle:** *Not* always be closing, but always be connecting.
3. **Using content as currency:** Sharing other people's useful content to help buyers solve problems—not narcissistic, self-absorbed content that's all about how great you are.
4. **Social listening for leads:** It can be difficult to listen for leads without organization redesign and support tools.
5. **Measuring what matters:** Deciding what metrics will best measure the impact social is having on your business. What indicators will you look for? How will you tie it to pipeline and revenue?

---

23 Iab.net. *IT Purchasing Goes Social*, 2012. http://www.iab.net/media/file/IT_Purchasing_Goes_Social-Best_Practices_Final.pdf (accessed February 10, 2015).

One of the most important pillars is Jill's third one, **using content as currency**. The traditional sales funnel should now look more like a content pipeline, yet that's often the hardest thing for sales professionals to master.

For me the three social platforms that make up my unified content pipeline are Twitter, LinkedIn, and Facebook, and moving someone through that pipeline is like peeling an onion. I get to know someone on Twitter by striking up a conversation. From there I move the relationship to an acceptance platform (LinkedIn) and deepen the sharing. Then as we get to know each other, we make it more personal by accepting each other as friends on Facebook.

It might seem that building this kind of personal branding takes too much time, especially if you're building it across multiple networks. Keeping track of all those conversations can seem like herding cats—but social CRM tools like Nimble can help us manage our connections across channels and not lose track of engagement opportunities.

Outside of sales teams, there are other ways businesses can be "social helpers," and one of them is participating in random acts of kindness. Here are some examples we've seen:

- Randomly delivering free meals to customers on their birthdays. (The restaurant Habana Cuba in San Jose does this. When you register your birthday with them, you're entered into a drawing.)
- @HiddenCash—AKA real estate developer and millionaire Jason Buzi became famous for hiding envelopes of cash around several cities in the US and posting clues on Twitter. The scavenger hunt came to San Jose and produced a frenzy! Everyone looked at each other with suspicion, wondering if they were standing next to the person responsible for hiding cash and dropping clues. Jason uses the power of social to "pay it forward," and

attributes the popularity of the hunts to people's love for puzzles combined with a desire to come together using social.

In a discussion about his book *Youtility: Why Smart Marketing Is About Help, Not Hype,* Jay Baer sums up social helping nicely:

> You're much better off as a brand (and frankly, as an individual) if you can use social media to promote your very useful information instead of using it to promote your products and services directly. This idea of "We're awesome, click here to let us prove it," which a lot of tweets, Facebook updates, and blog posts currently say, is not something someone will gravitate toward. We need to remember that if you sell something, you create a customer today; if you help someone, you create a customer for life.

Keeping the concept of helping in mind and using social tools to keep track of contacts, engagement opportunities, and goals is the best way to leverage the relationship building power of sharing. Now let's break this down further and delve into what constitutes a quality share.

CHAPTER 11

WHAT MAKES STUFF WORTH SHARING

Word-of-mouth communication is powerful. It's humankind's earliest form of sharing information. But what's the science and/or psychology behind it? I talked to Jonah Berger, marketing professor at the Wharton School and author of the *New York Times* bestseller *Contagious: Why Things Catch On*. Jonah has spent the last decade studying the science of word of mouth (WOM) and helping businesses apply those concepts to grow their brands. Finally, after a decade of blindly feeling our way around social media, because of Jonah's work we have an understanding of how online sharing works and how we can apply it to our businesses in a meaningful way.

A fact that came up in our conversation surprised me. According to research Jonah cites in his book, only 7 percent of WOM happens online. Does that surprise you? As connected as people are these days, I thought it would be around 50 percent (and others have guessed 30 to

70 percent), but this shows us how much impact our offline world has on what we share in social channels—it's more than we think.

So why does one brand get more WOM than another? How can you use those insights to make your content more contagious? According to Jonah, it's not random, and it's not luck. His studies revealed a number of key scientific principles that drive people to talk and share, and he identified six key drivers symbolized by the acronym STEPPS: **Social Currency, Triggers, Emotion, Public, Practical Value,** and **Stories.** No one step is more important than the others—no magic recipe will work the same for every business—and you don't need to apply all of them to every marketing effort. However, keeping these drivers in mind when creating content can certainly help you increase your batting average.

In our interview Jonah explained how he used some of the STEPPS principles in the creation and release of his book. For instance, he chose a cover design that was bright orange (keeping the public in mind), which is considered an attractive color that many people are likely to be curious about and talk about. Using the trigger concept, the book was released during cold and flu season along with orange tissues with messaging that said, "Don't you wish your idea was this contagious?" The tissues were a unique way to help people associate the book with the contagiousness of ideas. This kind of association is important in attaining WOM because if it's top of mind, it's tip of tongue. Like peanut butter and jelly, you can't mention one without thinking about the other.

What's a unique thing that will make people think about you often? What's your brand's peanut butter?

I asked Jonah what makes an incident stick in your mind and makes you want to share it. "Remarkability is one thing," he replied, and noted that it is a form of social currency (the first letter in STEPPS). As an example he talked about when he decorated his home for a party and supplied the bathrooms with black toilet paper. "Everyone's going to remember that black toilet paper—it's certainly different from anything else I had seen—and it makes people want to share it because they feel it makes them look cool and 'in the know' to remark on something like that."

As an exercise for this book, I analyzed my Facebook and Twitter streams to determine why some posts were more shared than others. Let's see how some top-performing posts stack up against Jonah's STEPPS drivers.

Facebook Posts: The posts pictured below are some that received good engagement on my personal profile in terms of comments and likes:

Bryan Kramer
April 25 near San Jose, CA

The last person to leave a comment here, I will send you a free signed copy of Human to Human #H2H. GO!

Like · Comment · Share   👍 35 💬 292

I think **practical** (or perceived) **value** is the driver for these high-comment numbers, don't you?

Bryan Kramer
June 19

One of the best parts of my night was not just a book signing but having my two high school English teachers attend! #H2H — with Anne Kline and Donna Dawson-Schwartz at Village House Of Books.

Like · Comment · Share

Ted Rubin, Jon Ferrara and 157 others like this.

View 27 more comments

Tessa Robinson Solley I love this photo. #gomustangs
June 19 at 3:44pm · Like · 👍 3

Brad Dodge Love it. You teachers are never forgotten.
June 19 at 4:17pm · Like · 👍 2

Karen Umberger Wonderful picture of my long time friend, Mrs. Kline, how proud you have made both teachers
June 19 at 7:01pm · Like · 👍 2

Everybody remembers their favorite teachers, and genuine smiles in this visual elicit a positive **emotional** response. There's also good **story** value here.

Bryan Kramer
April 18 near Palm Springs, CA

In my massage just now, the massage lady just pulled my leg over to stretch,
then she pushed from one side of the table to give me a really good stretch.
In theory, I think it could have worked. But she pushed too hard and I rolled
off the entire massage table.

Like · Comment · Share   👍 88 💬 53

Although some of my posts received more likes than
this one, the **story** is what drove the comments (plus it's
darned funny). Do you think it would have received more
engagement if there were a photo to go with the story?

Twitter: Tweets with the most RTs and Favorites (a quick analysis
using Twitonomy).

For Twitter, it looks like the remarkability (**social currency**) factor
of the "no more B2B or B2C" statement was high, although it was
higher the second time it was introduced (April 28) than the first time
(April 25). But it still did well in June (all were tweeted from events—all
had a photo attached).

Understanding what's relevant to my audience (the people factor)
helped with "What I hate most on #Twitter …" What Twitter power
user hasn't come up against that problem?

A good example of how I used a "trigger" concept is how I associated H2H (with "no more B2B or B2C") with the idea that as the tag grows across the Web and more people read the book, the stronger the association.

In addition to Jonah Berger's work with STEPPS, a host of other emotions influence why and what we share. While there is no definitive list of the spectrum of emotions, one popular one, from emotion expert Paul Ekman, contains six: **fear**, **anger**, **sadness**, **disgust**, **surprise**, and **joy**. These six have been found in every society worldwide and can be identified by people regardless of upbringing, culture, or experience. In fact, neuroscience has shown that every human's facial expressions reflect these emotions in the same way, regardless of race.

These emotions directly apply to how, what, why, when, and where people share in social as well. Here are Ekman's six emotional styles of sharing, applied to social:

Fear: Fear removes us from dangerous situations or into them. I know many people who are not on social media because they see social as an intrusion and fear as the repercussion of being social. I predict that this will change as Millennials grow up with a new set of social barriers.

Anger: Anger is an emotional response related to one's psychological interpretation of having been threatened. Some people are simply waiting on the sidelines to argue. Others take it further, becoming "haters" or "trolls." Anger is often one-sided unless it's accepted by both parties, in which case it's an endless quagmire of opinion-slinging, often only ending by "out-fatiguing" the other person.

Sadness: Sadness is an emotional pain associated with, or characterized by, feelings of disadvantage, loss, despair, helplessness, and sorrow. Bad things happen to good people, and sadness results. These experiences are shared often and typically draw an amazing support system. However, because sadness is not an activating, but a de-activating emotion, individuals and brands need to use it sparingly. There's solace in sharing our vulnerabilities and pain, and this can be quite healing, but content based on sadness won't be shared much if it becomes a crutch or part of one's social identity.

Disgust: Disgust is an emotional response toward something considered offensive or unpleasant. Social forms of disgust are varied, and often appear in the form of over-sharing or not thinking through who is reading your content. Others simply don't care when they share, or who they may hurt in sharing. As are the many decisions in life, we can take part in these discussions or just move on.

Joy: Joy indicates that we have done or witnessed something that enhances our well-being, and encourages us and others to aspire to greatness. It's not an accident that Facebook built your profile as a timeline of your life so you could share with others all your joyful experiences. It feels great to share joyous occasions and makes us feel good as humans to see others experiencing joy.

Surprise: Surprise indicates that something unexpected has occurred and prepares us (and those around us) to deal with it. The element of surprise, when done right, can be a marketer's best tactic. I'll say it in one word: Apple.

It's important that we also understand, as people running and representing brands, that when your emotional response resonates authentically, mirroring will most likely take place. Mirroring anyone's body language allows you to bond and build understanding. It is a powerful tool that we use instinctively without even being aware of it.

The most obvious forms of mirroring are yawning and smiling. When you see someone yawn, or even if you just read the word "yawn," you are likely to yawn immediately, or within the next thirty seconds.

This same concept has been proven to work online. An example of mirroring was reported by The A.V. Club in January 2012. In this example, Facebook adjusted its newsfeed algorithm for several hundred thousand users to assess the impact of the content of newsfeeds on viewers' emotional state.

The resulting paper,[24] published in The Proceedings of the National Academy of Sciences (PNAS), found that people mirror the positive or negative emotions that their friends express in their posts—all without the aid of nonverbal cues like body language or tone of voice.

Creepy, right? Still, the results are interesting. To pull this off, Facebook engineers tweaked what 600,000 users saw in their newsfeeds so they saw more posts that expressed positive emotions, while others saw more posts that conveyed negative feelings. The result? People actually responded in kind. Those who saw more "positive" posts responded more positively, while those who saw more "negative" posts responded with negative feelings.

The researchers called this effect an "emotional contagion," because they purported to show that our friends' words on our Facebook newsfeed directly affected our own mood (you can read more from *Forbes* on Facebook altering its algorithm here: http://www.forbes.com/ sites/jeffbercovici/2014/06/30/facebooks-experiment-on-emotions-sounds-creepier-than-it-was/). That said, it's ironic that the very study that sought to logically prove that emotions affect human behavior in social caused more emotional reactions than it measured.

---

24   Kramer AD, Guillory JE, Hancock JT. Experimental evidence of massive-scale emotional contagion through social networks. Proc Natl Acad Sci USA. 2014;111(24):8788-90.

Understanding the emotional underpinnings of sharing can be helpful in developing your sharing strategy, but that's only part of the picture. How do we put it to use from a practical marketing standpoint? How do we cut through the clutter to get seen and heard in the newsfeeds of our customers so they'll share what we have to say?

Content Marketing, Social Sharing, and the Rule of Thirds

Just a few short years ago "content marketing" was a new term instead of the business buzzword it's become. In the past, a company could get enough attention by regularly releasing white papers. Now, we know that to stand out, we need to do more. We need to become our own media companies and embrace social sharing. But what does that involve? What's the optimal mix?

If you're an investor in the stock market, you wouldn't dream of investing in just one stock or bond. A salesman wouldn't depend on one customer for their livelihood or they would be out of business.

The same is true when you're planning what you share online. You'll have much better results if you diversify and break down what you share by the rule of thirds (much the same way as an artist or a photographer breaks down their work). Break your shared content into three buckets: one-third news, one-third ideas, and one-third owned or curated content. Diversifying your content gives you a much better landscape for success. You'll always have variation without giving too much in any one area. This will open the perception of your brand in the social marketplace and give you more opportunities to help more people.

This applies to individuals as well as brands. If I just talk about my kids on Facebook, for instance, it gets annoying. And if people never see anything new or unique coming from you, the likelihood of them liking any of your posts will dwindle. In the absence of interaction, Edgerank takes over so people start seeing less of your posts, and you gradually fall off their radar altogether. On Twitter, people get unfollowed and unlisted when they become boring, annoying, offensive, or nonexistent. Online search is going in the same direction. Without publishing a variety of content types (audio, video, images, and written content), and getting other people to share them, brands are left out of organic search results.

The popularity of what you share follows relevance—the intersection of your message and audience interests at the moment in time they're experiencing it. Relevance isn't static—we talked earlier about the importance of context and how that affects the impact of what we share.

Employing sensory marketing can help improve the odds that you'll share information that is relevant to your audience. Some people are more visual, some prefer audio, some respond more to imagery and others to written content. Balancing out the forms of what you share (and repurpose) to cover more senses increases the likelihood that it will appeal to more kinds of people. You can't predict the outcome, but testing allows you to see pretty quickly what resonates, so you can tweak your content based on what works.

In a conversation with my friend DJ Waldow, former digital marketing evangelist at Marketo, and coauthor of *The Rebel's Guide to Email Marketing,* DJ and I discussed varying and testing content for his newsletter, especially the challenge to be more personal. Using video can be a way of varying the sensory appeal, and DJ spoke of the success he's had in experimenting with video in his newsletters:

> I've been trying something with my weekly newsletter lately where I do a little intro video, usually a couple minutes long. I'm either providing some sort of tip or something around email. I found when I first did that, a good 30 percent of my list of people who opened the email actually watched that entire video. Part of that was because it was new and because I used a human approach. I looked into the camera. I was talking to people on my list as if I knew them and said, "Here's an important tip for

you. Here's something to think about around email." A lot of people responded to that directly, and I had a dialogue and a conversation back and forth through email as a result. It was a different approach that resonated with my audience.

DJ also spoke about the challenges of making emails more personal and personable. "It's very easy to pull a list, your entire list, and create an email, and hit send," he said. The challenge with that is to survive what he calls the "inbox triage" that all of us practice when we look at our inboxes in the morning. "The more you can make that communication personalized to that person [so they feel] that it's really written for them by a human to another human, the better off you'll be," he noted.

A company whose messaging survives DJ's inbox triage is Upworthy, a media outfit that often uses a humorous approach with messaging like "Did you click this email because you're totally procrastinating on something you really have to do? Good. We won't tell. Take five minutes to enjoy. Doing stuff in a rush goes way faster anyway." Who wouldn't want to read the rest?

Speaking of emails, our inboxes are becoming so cluttered that we're losing track of important communications, but business communication as a whole is morphing as we speak, and smart companies are at the forefront with new innovations. For instance, IBM Verse is a new, collaborative blending of email and cognitive computing that helps people prioritize what's in their inbox to track and act upon it quickly. It's mail that understands you because analyzes how you interact with email to interpret what's most important to you. Innovations like Verse are changing the way people view email and will have a huge impact on the way we work and share (more on this in Chapter 14).

No matter what channels you use in content marketing, varying your approach to giving and sharing is important, but so is measuring your results. What's the yardstick you'll use? Sometimes we look at results as a bottom line number, a line item, or a dollar amount. With emails it's most likely open and click-thru rates, or the number of times the email was shared. In social media it could be impressions, reach, scores, referrals. It could be a thousand different things depending on your KPIs. Social media returns can happen in so many different ways that you can't define them as just one number.

Create a Content Strategy by Thinking Like a Media Company

Before we can implement a sharing strategy, it's important to have a content strategy in place to feed it. Current marketing wisdom indicates that to be seen and heard above the noise out there, consumers need to see, interact, or engage with our content three to five times. Why so many?

Back in Chapter 4 I mentioned Michael Brito's book *Your Brand: The Next Media Company*. In it he says our audience's universe and the way they absorb content has changed and that we need to change how we think about and produce content. In a webinar for PureMatter, Michael outlined five basic characteristics of the external market that are driving these changes:

1. **We live in a world of content/media surplus.** Outside of social, the average person sees three to six thousand marketing messages a day. It's very hard to rise above that kind of noise.
2. **Consumers have attention deficit.** We have a finite ability to absorb content and too many other things competing for our time. We have multiple devices. We multitask. Time is at a premium, so all content is filtered for the shorter attention span.
3. **The consumer's journey through life is dynamic and unpredictable.** How can you create and deliver valuable

experiences and content if you don't know where your consumers are or what time they're going to be there? How do you know when they are searching?

4. **People have tunnel vision.** Billboards, ads, and conversations are only relevant to us in specific moments in time. After that they just blend into our backgrounds. The attention deficit and content surplus make us tighten our focus so that the only things that jump out are the things that matter to us right now.

5. **Everyone is influential.** Social score metrics really don't matter. We all influence each other every day in one way or another.

There are two basic answers to these challenges: active listening (which we covered earlier) and creating more content based on what we're hearing. However, creating enough content and finding the time to do it is a huge challenge for marketers. According to the 2013 B2B Content Marketing Benchmarks, Budgets and Trends research report25 by Content Marketing Institute, 78 percent of marketers say this is their biggest hurdle. The same survey reports that 44 percent of marketers don't have a documented content strategy. So how do we change that?

When Michael Brito suggests that we think and act more like media companies, what does that mean? Well, media companies are set up to crank out content and surround their listeners with it. If you think about the likes of Time Warner, Comcast, or Condé Nast, that's their sole purpose—to create quality, relevant content and deliver it to their audiences. So as non-media companies, we need to "refit" our companies with a top-down social business framework that encompasses people, processes, and platforms.

---

25 Available at: http://www.slideshare.net/CMI/b2b-content-marketing-2013-benchmarks-budgets-and-trendsnorth-america-14855770. Accessed April 9, 2015.

How Can an Agency Support a Campaign, and How Do You Know When You Need One?

Content marketing is a beast that needs to be constantly fed. Unless you have a team to help you, you'll be swallowed up in the sheer volume, time, and energy it takes to produce really worthwhile content.

Sometimes, hiring an agency or team of writers to help is a good idea. But how do you know when you need help? Courtney explained it best during her segment on a recent #BizHeroes Tweetchat hosted by Kelly Hungerford from List.ly:

Q. How can an agency support a campaign and how do you know when you need one?

A: Well, that's like asking, "How do you know when it's time to stop making your own clothes and start buying at the store?"

Some people are really great at sewing their own clothes. They may be expert designers who have created a demand for what they're selling.

They've built a catwalk in their lobby! They don't need no stinkin' store.

But some people suck at sewing. They've been poked to death by needles. They run with scissors. They tried to make their own clothes but have learned the hard way that they're store people.

They're willing to spend the money on the clothes because they're sick of standing bloodied in their lobby. They get the value and can't wait to go shopping.

That's when a business knows they're ready to hire an agency. When they're naked and bleeding in their lobby.

Seriously, when a company realizes what they're doing in-house just isn't working, and they have the budget, resources, and energy to put into an agency relationship, that's the time to outsource.

Leveraging the Crowd

The last hurdle in making our content contagious is the people part— getting our content to spread among the largest crowd possible and catch on. In his interview with me, Jay Baer stated that "content is the match and social is the fire."

So let's think about a typical crowd for a moment. What constitutes a crowd, anyway? Social identity theory posits that the self is a complex system made up primarily of the concept of membership or non-membership in various social groups. Based on the personal values and morals of an individual, they will identify as a member or nonmember of an ambiguous crowd. This says to me that people feel like they either belong to a crowd or they don't.

Now let's look at a crowd of people who feel like they belong together. They've identified themselves as a member of this crowd, such as a sports stadium full of fans. When you're in a stadium enjoying a game, what makes a "wave" take off? By definition, a wave is a disturbance that travels through a medium. It only takes one person to start it, but there seems to be an invisible force that compels people to participate. Context, timing, and atmosphere all play a role.

The same analogy can be made about the social sphere. Like water, social media is also a medium, so like a wave in water, ideas make their way through the connected Internet much in the same way. In this case, the ideas are the energy force. The strength of the idea determines the speed that it travels across channels and how disruptive it is to its environment.

What kind of energy does it take to make a wave go around once, versus two, three, or even ten times? That's the potential power of crowd marketing on social channels? If you think of all the social channels that are available to us as a stadium of fans (around 750 of them, give or take), and an idea as the catalyst for a wave, imagine the power that could generate!

Using Brian Solis's Conversation Prism that illustrates the social platforms and how they're interconnected creates a "Social Stadium" for idea waves to pass around.

Social and digital technologies allow us to use the power of crowds in ways never before possible for cocreating content, for crowdsharing, and even crowdfunding. But the common denominator in the power of a crowd is shared emotion—something that connects us.

In *H2H* I referenced a great example of the viral nature of a shared emotion, the Batkid story from the Make-a-Wish Foundation of the Greater Bay Area in San Francisco. Miles Scott, a child who suffers from leukemia and loves Batman, wished to be Batkid for a day. The Make-a-Wish Foundation, with the help of the San Francisco Tribune and the San Francisco Giants, planned to transform San Francisco into Gotham City for Miles. A blogger picked up the story and posted it on Reddit two weeks before the event, and people started sharing it. And sharing it. And sharing it! Two weeks before the event, the blog on Reddit had over seventy thousand Likes. What began as a small effort to make a five-year-old boy a hero for the day turned into a national extravaganza. One person volunteered their Lamborghini as the Batmobile. Others volunteered to play roles in the storyline. It got so big they had to turn many volunteers away.

On the day of the event, not only were the streets of San Francisco flooded with well-wishers who held signs, dressed in costume, and cheered little Miles on as he made his way around town, the social sphere was watching in real time, tracking the experience. There were tweets from Ben Affleck, the Harlem Globetrotters—even a video from President Obama encouraging Miles to catch that villain! The president's tweet was retweeted over eight thousand times that day alone.

The Secrets to Making Something Crowdworthy

You've created some great content. You have a plan and the team to execute it. But how do you know if your work will be crowdworthy? I prefer this term over "going viral" because it puts the power into the hands of the people sharing it instead of celebrating the genius behind the person who created it. As I discussed in Chapter 8, sometimes what people deem crowdworthy is just stupid. Or it's shocking. Or it was a captured shared moment. The point is, people deem something crowdworthy when it connects with their humanity; others share it because it connects with theirs, and so forth.

I realize that "humanity" is a very broad criterion to determine if your next campaign is crowdworthy. Last year, after DJ Waldow, his wife, Kristina, and Courtney and I ran our #90DaystoEllen campaign and wrote about it in *H2H*, a lot of people wanted to know why that effort was so successful from a crowdworthiness perspective (you can still check out the site at www.90DaystoEllen.com if you want to read the whole story). We started looking at the campaign and other successful crowdworthy campaigns like Batkid and last summer's #ALSIceBucketChallenge

experience to see if we could spot some patterns. We found some pretty amazing things. We identified four common elements from each campaign that, if you applied to your campaign, would most likely make it crowdworthy. We still use this methodology for our campaigns at PureMatter, and it hasn't let us down yet.

You can view "Four Secrets to Making Something Crowdworthy" on YouTube at https://www.youtube.com/watch?v=rre27YE6JJQ. However, here they are in a nutshell:

Secret #1: Have a simple human concept.

Make a boy's wish come true.

Delight your customers.

Prove a point.

Secret #2: Have a structured plan.

Use a calendar.

Get a team behind you.

Know your end goal.

Secret #3: Invite people to the party.

Ask people to help.

Make it simple to share.

Reward and thank them.

Secret #4: Apply the rules of improv.

Say "yes" to ideas from the crowd.

Timing is everything.

Have fun with it.

An analysis of the recent ALS Ice Bucket Challenge experience that swept the world provides some lessons in how to apply these secrets. You have to have literally been just born or living on a remote desert island to have not heard about this event, but as a brief overview, as part of the challenge, people filmed themselves dumping buckets of ice cold water over their heads to inspire others to donate money to finding a cure for ALS. Many attribute the challenge's origins to Boston College when teammates of former Boston College baseball player Pete Frates, who was diagnosed with ALS in 2012, videoed themselves dumping ice water over their heads to raise awareness about the disease.

And here's what we found when we used our four secrets:

Secret #1: Did it have a simple concept?

Yes: Dump ice over your head. Donate.

Secret #2: Was there a plan?

In this case, the plan was the strong call to action for the challenge: Challengees had twenty-four hours to complete their ice bucket dump.

Secret #3: Did it invite people to the party?

Yes—in fact, this was one of the strongest pieces to create "members" of the campaign. In each video, three people were nominated to also take part. Videos were shared across social, and friends watch video. If you watched any of these videos, I am sure you were just waiting for someone you knew to challenge you (and it was only a matter of time.)

Secret #4: Did it apply the rules of improv?

Yes! This was a living, breathing, morphing beast of a campaign as it traveled over time. People had lots of fun with tons of humor. New charities were added beyond ALS. Group challenges started emerging in addition to individuals; entire NFL teams were challenging other teams together!

Okay, okay, so if you're a pragmatic numbers person you're asking yourself, "So the ALS Ice Bucket Campaign passed the crowdworthiness test. But what about the final results?"

The facts don't lie. As of September 2014:

- Over $100M raised
- Over 3 million donors from almost every country in the world in just two months
- Between June 1 – September 1, more than 17 million videos related to the Ice Bucket Challenge were shared on Facebook
- These videos were viewed more than 10 billion times on Facebook and reached more than 440 million people
- Celebrities and the rest of us were all equalized—we're all humans. I really liked this aspect of the campaign. I can't

remember another time when celebrities were able to show their human side and just be people. Newsflash ... celebrities shriek and shiver just like the rest of us when a freezing cold bucket of ice gets poured over their heads. This is what made it so fun and made me at least feel a connection to and endeared to many of these larger-than-life personalities.

The #ALSIceBucketChallenge "Social Stadium"

Although the ALS Ice Bucket Challenge was a success, it's important to show the flipside of crowdworthiness—when the crowd turns against you. Because of the popularity of the challenge, many brands thought that growth hacking some of its popularity was a good idea. One of those brands was Samsung, which mimicked the premise of the challenge (pouring water over your head) in a TV spot to demonstrate spot the waterproof quality of its new phone. The crowd spotted the inappropriateness of this a mile away and took to Twitter to mock the attempt.

Some thought it was genius. Some thought it was crass. The point is that it was a "flash in the pan." People moved on and forgot about it.

Never choose being "clever"—what Samsung thought it was being—over empathy.

Cocreating Content with Crowdsourcing

In the Digital Age, anything can be crowdsourced—designs, book ideas, wikis (like Wikipedia), work projects, and more. In fact, I often crowdsource my blog articles by first asking questions about the topic on my social channels the day before. This gives me immediate responses that help shape my content and test the message. Multiple heads are definitely better than one, and the content developed from these efforts is often superior to what I would create by myself.

Creating content is one of the easiest things to crowdsource. Encouraging comments on your blog, taking advantage of polls, and/or creating an influencer marketing strategy are just a few ways you can crowdsource content ideas and creation.

Today's mobile technologies also allow us to cocreate video content, such as the Hollywood & Vines campaign by Airbnb, a first-of-its-kind short film created from six-second Vine videos submitted from all over the world. Airbnb asked their Twitter audience to answer one question a day using Vine, which resulted in over 750 entries in six days. These were then pieced together with a music background to create a compelling visual story about travel, adventure, and finding your place in the world. The desire to belong and to participate in something is very powerful, which is what made this video such a success. The film received over 342,000 views on YouTube and was one of the most shared videos on Mashable.

The Growth of Crowdfunding

While crowdsharing and crowdsourcing are big ways to leverage the power of crowds for spreading content, the ultimate success story is crowdfunding. Just type the term "crowdfunding" into Google, and you'll get more than eight million results! Raising money for various causes and business opportunities has never been so easy, and startups like Indegogo, GiveForward, and Kickstarter top the search results, with more cropping up on a seemingly daily basis. This is yet another disruptive business model fueled by mobile and social technologies, and it's surprising how fast it has taken off. As of 2013 the Crowdfunding Industry Report (yes, there's a crowdfunding industry!) put the total proceeds generated from crowdfunding at just over $5 billion. However, a new report by infoDev for the World Bank26 indicates that the annual market potential for the global crowdfunding industry (which now includes equity firms) could reach $300 billion by 2025.

I'm sure you can see from our discussions in these chapters (and from looking back at your own experiences) how important sharing is to everything we undertake. I've been studying the art and science of sharing for quite a while, and it's a fascinating journey that's far from over. In researching *Shareology* I've had the pleasure of talking with dozens of experts and brands on the topic and have highlighted a few great examples in the next chapter, "Brands on Sharing."

---

26   Best, Jason, Neiss, Sherwood, Swart, Richard. "Crowdfunding's Potential for the Developing World." 2013. *infoDev, Finance and Private Sector Development Department. Washington, DC: World Bank.*http://www.infodev.org/infodev-files/infodev_crowdfunding_study_0.pdf (accessed February 15, 2015)

CHAPTER 13

BRANDS ON SHARING

S haring greatly impacts your reputation as a brand—what you share as a company, as well as what others share about you. So how can you do a better job of brand building through sharing? We talked to several companies about what they consider to be most important in building their online brands, what has been most successful for them, and some lessons other businesses can learn from their experiences. These are their stories. Enjoy!

Jay Curley from Ben & Jerry's on Telling the Brand Story

The following excerpt comes from a webinar, *Creating Authentic Experiences27*, conducted with Jay Curley for PureMatter.

For us, marketing is really about expressing ourselves as people and connecting with people who have shared values and shared experiences.

---

27   http://www.purematter.com/resource/webinar-replay-creating-authentic-experiences/

That's how we have built the B&J brand over the years. We try our best to cultivate our fanbase and deliver amazing experiences for them. We try to treat our fans the right way, as friends, whether it's at an event, in a scoop shop that you walk into or in an online community—wherever it might be.

We try to bring the full expression of our company to life in order to create authentic experiences.

Our mission statement promotes the idea of linked prosperity, which means that as the company succeeds, everyone the company touches should succeed equally. So instead of looking at a supply chain and trying to figure out how to extract as much value out of it as possible, we look at a supply chain and try to figure out how we can use the business to put value back into those communities. That starts mainly from where we get our ingredients, such as the dairy farms here in Vermont. We also source most of our commodities (such as sugar, cocoa, vanilla and coffee) through fair trade certified cooperatives, so it's about giving back to those communities. Then we think about where we live and work, and how we can give back to communities like that. And last, where we sell our products (which is thirty-plus countries). When we look at a community such as a city, we want to understand it so that we can provide value. We do the same thing when we look at emerging social communities like Instagram. How are we uniquely positioned to provide value to that community?

Ben & Jerry's is more of a values-led lifestyle company versus a CPG brand. We stand for a lot of things and are a multilayered company. It's not just about making the best ice cream.

Instagram Connection: We joined Instagram in 2011 and realized that we could really connect with people there and tell our story. We started sharing photos there, but very quickly understood that people loved sharing their photos with us. So we began thinking of ways we could thank our Instagram community. What value could we bring to them? We devised a program called #captureeuphoria that recognized amazing photography (which is very important to that community), and also gave people an opportunity to be recognized for their photography. We asked them to share their euphoric moments with us. These moments weren't all about ice cream—it was whatever euphoria meant to individuals. We created one-off advertisements in local communities of about eight different countries that featured the winner's user name and photo and thanked them for participating. We did billboards, newspaper ads, even special coasters for one community.

Twitter Connection: In 2013 we found that there were thousands of people who tweeted that they were spending their Valentine's Day alone with Ben & Jerry. So we put together a Twitter campaign and sent out personalized Valentine tweet cards to every person who mentioned Ben & Jerry's on Valentine's Day. Each was unique. The next year we sent about sixty ice cream cakes to people in four cities. Both of these campaigns allowed us to listen to our community and connect with people when they were thinking about us.

We start with stories and information, and out of those build content for the digital world and experiences for the real world.

What's our philosophy on changing social platforms? We always look at what's new and ask, "Does it make sense for us to use this platform?" It's still all about bringing value to a particular space. For brands, the biggest challenge is deciding how you're going to break through. It all comes back to asking yourself how you can make your story relevant to that space. Moving forward, learning to adapt to evolving technologies will change the way we connect with people and tell our story.

Mark Waxman, CMO of CBIZ Inc.

We asked Mark how highly regulated professional services can do the best job of sharing in today's social world, and here's what he had to say:

It comes down to two things:

1. On the front end, do a good job of defining what you can and cannot discuss. Publicly traded companies, for instance, cannot share company performance on social channels. Coach individuals on what they can share—like their expertise—and what they absolutely have to stay away from. There are also HIPPA laws for insurance companies, so you need to proactively identify what's allowed and give them specific guidelines.
2. Help provide your people with shareable content (curated and otherwise) that has already gone through these channels. This will help them with their comfort level.

[Additionally], teach your people the social media fundamentals and create your own content to do so. These can be webinars, videos, etc., but in small, modular segments—fifteen or thirty minutes—so they can work that into their schedules and short attention spans. At CBIZ, we get much higher engagement with content we create that's made for them and their peers rather than third party content.

We also developed a hands-on workshop that we do at large events. We'll park our social media experts in the foyer of the event for one-on-one help and training and gamify it to encourage participation with a contest—giving away an iPad or iPhone or another technology product. They get expert help in setting up their profiles, setting up groups, getting content—whatever they need to be successful.

Reward your employees for their social activity and recognize social media stars publicly (who has the most tweets, the most shares, etc.). Get the word out in multiple ways, starting with your own intranet, social channels, and emails, and hand out physical recognition (such as plaques) at company events.

Royal Dutch Airlines KLM Touches Heartstrings

What's more emotional than saying goodbye to loved ones at the airport? Recognizing the power of emotional connection to influence brand sentiment, the Dutch airline KLM allowed friends and family members to write special messages to their departing loved ones, and then quickly attached those messages to the headrests of their seats before they boarded the plane. Called "Cover Greetings," this specialized customer-service campaign took a bit of scrambling at the airport—but the ensuing goodwill it created among passengers was well worth the effort. See the YouTube video KLM produced here: http://youtu.be/ DH8D2OHn18c.

According to an online travel article in the *Daily Mail*,[28] people had this to say about the campaign:

Ryan Owiti wrote: "That's So Special and Awesome!! I love it!! That's why I love KLM and the rest of the Sky Team. Cannot wait to travel KLM again!!

"Whenever you think that does not get better, KLM comes and goes one better," wrote Jakob Ruprecht. "Even if this is just a one-time action for the filming of a promotional film, the idea is compelling."

---

28 http://www.dailymail.co.uk/travel/travel_news/article-2850673/KLM-tug-heartstrings-delivering-surprise-greetings-loved-ones-passengers-board-flight. html#ixzz3L2ja1Ad2

Arturo Eggler wrote: "It's about how you make your customers
feel.... Great campaign KLM!!!"

In addition to Cover Greetings, another customer-led strategy
the airline employed involved treating a newlywed couple to an
express trolley drive (trailing tin cans and sporting a "Just Married"
sign) to board their plane. These strategies were part of their Twitter
#HappyToHelp campaign.

Yet another campaign, an earlier one, the KLM Lost & Found[29]
service at Amsterdam Airport Schiphol, used a trained dog, Sherlock, to
reunite passengers with lost items.

Are these campaigns publicity stunts? Perhaps, but I'll argue that the
emotions engendered by the videos are real and definitely have a positive
impact on the brand. Check out KLM's Twitter Page for more fun ways
the brand engages customers.

---

29 KLM Lost & Found Service Video: https://www.youtube.com/watch?v=NK-T_
    t166TY

The Quirky Momma Story

Michael Stelzner told us about this one. Holly Homer and Rachel Miller partnered to create kidsactivitiesblog.com for parents who love kids' art, crafts, games, food, and learning activities. They also cowrote a book for this niche, *101 Kids Activities That Are the Bestest, Funnest Ever!*[30]

To grow an audience, the pair worked to develop a Facebook page and within nine months had organically amassed over 645,000 likes by sharing content that goes viral quickly. Their purpose was to drive traffic to their blog and promote their book, and their social media efforts have been a huge success, as indicated by the following chart:

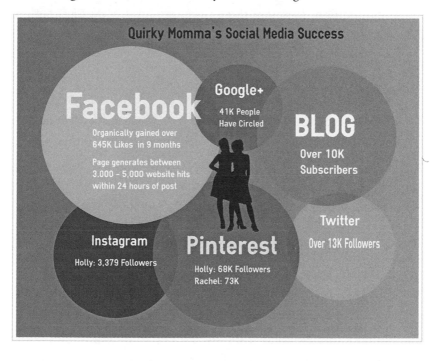

Quirky Momma's Social Media Success

Facebook
Organically gained over 645K Likes in 9 months

Page generates between 3,000 – 5,000 website hits within 24 hours of post

Google+
41K People Have Circled

BLOG
Over 10K Subscribers

Instagram
Holly: 3,379 Followers

Pinterest
Holly: 68K Followers
Rachel: 73K

Twitter
Over 13K Followers

---

30   Holly Homer, Rachel Miller, *101 Kids Activities That Are the Bestest, Funnest Ever!* (Page Street Publishing, 2014)

These ladies learned some pretty cool things about sharing as they developed their social presence and have never advertised to grow their fanbase. Michael Stelzner interviewed Holly, and here are some excerpts from that conversation:

We had a Facebook page for several years, but it wasn't driving traffic. Nobody was clicking through or doing anything.

My blogging partner, Rachel, gets crazy ideas. She said, "Let's get fifty thousand fans by Christmas, because the book's coming out (*101 Kids Activities*) in spring. If we had fifty thousand fans, that would be cool." She started posting more and working with the page. We decided to emulate other successful pages, such as Happy Wives Club, but failed miserably. That's when I realized that this Facebook thing is really dependent on your fans!

Then a strange thing happened on our blog. A prominent Facebook page started stealing Kids Activities Blog content (without linking or attributing it to us) and posting it on their page, where the content went viral. They would grab a picture from one of our blog posts (cropping out our watermark) and use some of the content in the description, and it would get seven to nine thousand shares. I realized then that my content *could* be viral, but until that point Facebook had never proven that to me.

Those stolen images made us go back to our blog and do some digging. We found out which posts were being shared the most on other social media sites like Pinterest to get a baseline for what kind of content was most shareable and posted those on Facebook. At that point we were sharing mostly our own stuff, but as our page started to grow, we started to find other cool content to share as well and started fitting that in. Our ratio of posts now is one-third our content and two-thirds curated content. One of the strategies when you're growing your page and you want to increase the exposure of your posts is to curate content from a page that has a bigger People Talking About This (PTAT) percentage than you do. You'll get some of that Facebook karma when you share those. The same applies to tagging. If you're going to tag a page in a post, always tag pages with higher PTAT numbers.

Diving into how Facebook decides how many people get to see something is at the root of success. I try to work back from the exposure number, find several posts with the same exposure number, and figure out how it was achieved. One example is a post I wrote that was shared less than ten times on the page. When I dug deeper into Insights, that post actually had an exposure to nearly 200,000 people. How? The key was that people clicked through. Whether it's a like or a comment, share or click, all those things add up.

Rachel and I are addicted to analytics, so we would post and then watch the insights. Whatever post got engagement, we copied the format and style for another post like it. I also loved the way Google Plus lets you format your posts with bold and italic fonts. Facebook doesn't, and the posts looked ugly, so I experimented and redesigned our FB posts with a headline in all caps, then double-spaced and put in the link, then double-spaced again and put in a chatty little description. That style works so well we use it on virtually all of our posts now. Those are things that we learned by watching what happened in analytics.

When you're starting out, a good process is to create the page you want. Forget about insights for two weeks. Just create the best page you can. Share your best and brightest, the best stuff you have online. After that two-week period, go back to Insights and see what was working and what wasn't for that period. Get a baseline for how an average post should perform. Then moving forward, mimic the ones that do well.

Building Your Personal Brand

Jill Rowley told us (in Chapter 10) that building a personal brand and showing up in social networks the right way—in a human way—is one of the first pillars of social selling. Whether you're creating a business brand or you're just being yourself, your "brand" is your uniqueness—your personality—what makes you different from all the other people out there who do the thing(s) you do.

As with everything we've talked about in this book, building your personal brand starts with knowing your audience and being clear on the intrinsic value you bring to that audience. What makes you better than anyone else in your niche? What is it about you that resonates with people?

Let's dissect a few personal brands as examples. For instance, **James Franco** is a famous celebrity among the Millennial crowd. Outside of his films, he built a social persona of a narcissistic, self-serving guy that his audience finds very funny (especially on Instagram). Unlike other celebrities, who tend to want to keep themselves out of the spotlight outside their work, James is a power user of Instagram, using the visual platform to build a tongue-in-cheek social brand that looks like "my life as a movie." This is a brilliant move that not only resonates with his audience, but differentiates him from other celebrities.

George Takei is another good celebrity example. His funny, quirky sense of humor and his outspokenness on gay rights influences what he shares online. He's careful not to let his *Star Trek* roots define him, and he shares a variety of things that lots of people find interesting, with a healthy peppering of "Oh Myyyy!" posts, his trademark for sometimes risqué humor. George definitely has personality, and it shines through in what he shares.

If you're looking for an entrepreneurial personal brand with panache, look no further than **Richard Branson** on LinkedIn. One of LinkedIn's top influencers, Branson posts once or twice a month. He covers just about every aspect of independent thinking, from describing his first job (breeding budgerigars when he was eleven), to productivity hacks, the state of government today, tips on finding a fulfilling career, starting a company—even writing about famous personalities he admires. But if you look at the titles, the common thread is living life (and conducting business) to the fullest. He freely shares his success secrets, encourages people to be themselves and not be afraid to take the tiger by the tail, and is always upbeat and positive. His brief experience description as founder of Virgin Group is a perfect outline of his brand personality: tie-loathing adventurer and thrill seeker who believes in turning ideas into reality. Otherwise known as Dr. Yes at Virgin!

Building a personal brand isn't just important for celebrities and high-profile business owners, however. As you've no doubt seen throughout this book, each of us has influence within our own tribes, and what and how we share with them ripples across the universe to touch people in ways we could never imagine possible. That's why it's important for businesses to recognize that power among their employees and to nurture it. We can do so much more for our companies if we empower every individual within them to build a personal brand and share from it. But we're not quite there yet. It's going to "take a village" to make the mindset shift necessary for businesses to embrace this concept. However, as new technologies continue to shape the way we connect and communicate, we'll see this happen on a much larger scale.

What does the future hold? I talked to a number of social and business experts to glimpse into their crystal balls and have outlined their predictions in the next chapter.

CHAPTER 14:
THE SHARING FUTURE: WHAT'S NEXT?

Charline Li, Altimeter Group, on the Future of Branding:

The future depends on us thinking about individual and corporate brands living together in harmony. When we talk about a brand we're also talking about the people inside the brand and the experiences they have and want to share. So companies need to highlight the individual's brand as well as their own.

Individual brands are a fantastic thing. And frankly, we could not attract the top thought leaders if they ever thought that their personal brand would suffer at the benefit of a corporate brand. Companies need to invest in both because when I amplify and make you look good, you're going to make me look good too. We're all going to rub off on each other and raise the tide together.

Jeff Schick, GM of Social Software at IBM, on the Future of Email:
Email is one of the most important collaborative applications that people use, and industry leaders at innovative companies, like Jeff Schick of IBM, are working to improve the email experience. I spoke with Jeff about the future of work and email. Although email hasn't changed much since its inception, I was excited to learn that IBM is taking steps to address some of email's biggest challenges. For example, making it actionable, getting rid of clutter, and bringing things that are important to me to the front of the pile.

Jeff described the typical problems most of us face when confronting our email inboxes. "When I come in in the morning, first thing I do is go to my email and open it," he said. "By the time I'm done at the end of the day, I may have twenty to thirty emails still unopen. I started opening them up, and either someone asked me to do something, or I needed somebody to go do something for me—but if I didn't dispatch that email or get around to answering it, it went into my monolithic follow-up folder."

If your inbox looks like mine, it feels more like a Twitter stream, which makes it difficult to find things. Jeff shared that new approaches to email include addressing prioritization (so you can immediately get to what's important to you), better search (so you can find not just emails, but attachments, links, people, and calendar invites), integration with file sharing and syncing, and smarter analytics that eliminate the myriad steps you have to take to manage email while delivering more targeted information. In essence, email is changing to bring social, email, and mobile technologies together in a unified approach. It's about time!

What exciting things does he see coming down the pike concerning email?

"The role of cognitive computing will provide a path to better collaboration in email," he told me. "For example, in the collaboration space we've ingested the corpus of knowledge about all of the collaboration capabilities and products; so if I'm sitting in my inbox and I have a question about something related to that, I can get the answer (with 98 percent accuracy) to my specific problem right away. I'm not waiting ten minutes or an hour or two for a response; I'm getting a response in subseconds or within a minute. When you open the aperture of that corpus to include other data types, there is unlimited potential—unlocking information delivery capabilities that allow you to get the right information into the right hands and the right time to yield the right result. That's where we're headed."

Jay Baer on the Future of Content Sharing:
You're going to see a lot more integration at the execution level. You'll have software platforms that allow you as an individual or as a brand to create content, to test content, to optimize content, and then promote and amplify that content all in one place.

It's not dissimilar from what Google Ad Words has today. You see some companies already sort of approaching that in the space. That dashboard platform that does-it-all will be something that I think will take a lot of pain out of the game.

The reality of that is that social media has gone from art to science. This notion of "I'm a community manager, and I just have a good instinct for people," and "I'm a good writer and people like me," is being replaced by, "Hey, I can actually analyze a whole bunch of data and figure out what works and figure out that we've got to be sending this out at 2:11 instead of 2:22."

There's a lot more detail to this than there used to be. The same thing happened in email, the same thing happened in SEO, the same thing happened in banners. It's a natural evolution of new marketing tactics, where it starts off as an art and then starts to become a science when it gets more competitive.

Kare Anderson on the Future of Sharing in Leadership:

The hardest thing for leaders is to give up secondary goals to be really clear about the top goals they want for their company and themselves. The more distinctive and specific they are, the more interesting, understandable, and memorable they are. I believe that at least 90 percent of companies (and probably more) still struggle with internal battles and give out mixed messages because the top management has not agreed on the differentiating benefit.

So if you want to lead your company by example, then be clear on your own brand and share that clarity with everyone in your organization. Be distinctive and make references to people in other professions and industries where you compare your differentiating benefit as an individual and as a company to theirs—attractive comparisons. Be so distinctive that you create the playing field on which competition and collaboration happens because whoever most vividly characterizes a situation determines how other people see it in their mind's eye and act on it.

Mari Smith on the Future of Brand Shareability:

Brands will come out from their corporate structure and realize more and more that the audience is not connecting with the logo or the building or even the shape of the product; that ultimately, they just want to belong.

They want to belong to fan clubs with other people that love the brand. More emphasis will be made on "storifying" the brand and creating great experiences for people because when that happens, a brand's customers will share it with their audiences and with their circle of friends.

Matt Cohen on the Future of Content Marketing and Advertising:
Content marketing will become more ubiquitous. It's already the number one focus for digital marketers, but most of them are still in the early stages of adoption. You're going to see an increasing adoption, as well as an increasing sophistication and codification of best practices like you've seen with a number of other digital marketing techniques.

You're also going to see the native advertising space look more like other kinds of advertising. The lines are going to start blurring between what is a native ad, what is a regular ad, and what is a content ad. We'll see an explosion of options. Native advertising is really more where mobile was three, four, five years ago. Then you're going to see a consolidation and a specialization, where some of the players will drop out. Some will focus on very specialized customers. Then the rest will start to roll up. You'll see a few, new big players emerge. A lot of the recognizable names will take a significant part of the business as well.

Mike Stelzner, founder of Social Media Examiner,
on the Future of Social Platforms:
We're starting to see all of the platforms essentially becoming broadcast publications. They're becoming like television, radio, or email. Where I see things going is it's much more about delivering valuable content via the platform—Twitter, Facebook, LinkedIn, Google Plus, whatever it is—and much less about the social component.

We're seeing this come alive with a lot of these advertising options, which are more of a broadcasting concept. So unfortunately, the "social" in social media is becoming irrelevant. More and more brands are pushing content out and not engaging with audiences because the networks are essentially enabling that by allowing them to pay just to push. Pay to push is the future.

What this means is that brands with money can just bypass the work and pay to get their message out. The downside to this is that it could result in people fleeing from social networks. People came to the social networks, historically, to engage and to discover things about their family. If brands are no longer incentivized to engage, but instead they're given a path to push for money, they will always opt to push. It's much more costly to hire personnel and staff all over the world to engage and answer people's questions.

What we're going to see is that the social networks will become ghost towns eventually because only those social networks that actually try to hold up a bit of truism and reward brands not for just putting out content that everyone likes to share, but actually reward them for interacting with their clients.

Currently, there is no reward for true engagement. Facebook rewards stuff that goes viral, not stuff that has any level of engagement from the page itself. As long as that's the case, that means that more and more junk is going to be in our newsfeed. Whether it be a BuzzFeed thing that's designed to compel people psychologically to click, or whether it be a paid advertisement. As more and more junk gets into Twitter, LinkedIn, Facebook, Google Plus, and every other network that's out there, people will flee to other alternatives that are more pure and more social. This will be a never-ending system. I fear that's what's coming.

Nathan Latka of Heyo on Rising above the Noise:

The only thing I know for certain is that nothing will be the same. What that means is that there's going to be more content, especially with all these tools that are helping people create more content. So, you're still going to have to figure out how to rise above the noise. That's the key.

The only way to rise about the noise is by connecting human to human and understanding people on an emotional, empathetic level. That's something that tools can't replicate, and it's the ultimate driver that enables you to go from one to three to ten to twenty. Understand people at an emotional level, what they need, and give that to them via your content, and your content will supersede all the noise. Getting closer to your customers and your fans, understanding them better and engaging in real relationships—that's really what the future is.

Frank Eliason, CEO of CitiBank, on the Future of Adding Individual Value:

What we've seen up to now, for most companies, is mass marketing shifting into social media, which isn't adding value in the world. The future will be all about creating shareable moments. That's what social has been about all along, but companies consistently get it wrong. In fact, I think we'll see more companies getting out of social media sites because nobody cares what a company tweets or posts; we know it's intended for the masses.

What I see happening is that companies (especially banks) will create content that adds value to your life, and they'll direct that content to you as an individual. Social adds to the amount we know about you and what is concerning you and we'll continue to listen there. So the next time you log into our website to do your banking, we can deliver content that is relevant to your life right now. The hope is that by the time you need a mortgage, we're top of mind because we have been adding value to your life all along.

Sam Fiorella, Author of Influencer Marketing, on the Future of Measuring Influence:

For me, the current stage of change is to not focus on the growth of communities but to identify the relationship between the people within the communities. That means quantifying them better, segmenting them better, and then understanding the one-to-one relationship in terms of what I share and what I try and present to people in terms of forms of advertising as opposed to mass communications.

When digital came along we quickly turned to the Klout type programs and the mentality where people with the biggest voice, the biggest followers, were deemed influential.

Technology is allowing us to analyze the data, the social conversations, in such a way that we can focus on the context of what's being said; and by focusing on what is being shared as opposed to how much is being shared or how far that's being shared, I think influence marketing is going to grow in relevancy simply because we can better quantify the context or the result of what's being shared.

Author Shel Israel on the Movement of the "Freaky" Line:

Technology has always caused people to be uncomfortable, and the "freaky line" is the point at which we recoil from the benefits of technology. For instance, there were people who would not ride in automobiles when they first came out because they weren't horses. That was their freaky line. There was a reason why the early auto manufacturers started talking about horsepower because it was a unit of measure that people could understand. When you and I hear "300 horsepower," today we don't think of horses. We think about a big piece of iron that has nothing to do with horses.

The Internet, social media, mobile phones—everyone has their own freaky line when it comes to adoption of these new technologies and what we're willing to share with companies to benefit from those technologies. For example, if you go to a store or a tavern where you've never been before, and if you walk in and the barkeeper says, "Hello, Bryan. Oh, yeah, that's Bryan with a Y, not that other guy. Let me remember, you want a Manhattan, but you want it with one of those cute pink umbrellas in it, isn't that right?"

If you've never been in there before, you might be freaked out by this phenomenon. But ten years from now or twenty years from now, you will be very surprised if you walk into any retail store that hasn't used loyalty programs and contextual technologies to know exactly who you are and exactly why you've come into the store. And probably, they are ready to offer you a good price on the blue jeans you want or the semiautomatic weapon or whatever. As things move forward, I think the motion of the freaky line will become more interesting.

Author Robert Scoble on the Future of Technology and Sharing:
There are new social networks coming—networks that know you're hanging out with five people at a bar or if you're at a conference where there can be automatic hashtagging, and on and on. Certainly we are going to have wearable computers, whether it's a watch or a glass with a camera on it that'll let me capture more images or more video and share that.

People love sharing stuff with others, but there definitely is a push back to new technologies, which brings out new kinds of businesses. Snapchat has messages that disappear as soon somebody reads them, which came about because lots of people don't want to deal with the social consequences of sharing something (or even worse, having something, even in a private group, that has likes on it).

When I talk about context and this surveillance society that we're heading into, people say, "Man that freaks me out." But people are still going to use it because there is going to be deep utility for using it. It's just like most people use credit cards. That was the largest gifting for private information to a public company the world has ever seen. Yes, there are downsides to that, but the utility outweighs them. As long as there's utility, I believe people are going to use sharing technology.

Liz Urheim, VP of Collaboration Solutions at IBM,
on the Future of Work:

The future of work is going to be about the individual professional. It's no longer about the hierarchy of C-suite and management; it's no longer about structured reporting chains or processes about how you get your work done. Work is going to be very much a personal and personalized experience; who you are, what you do, how you work, what you like to do, and how you engage within your role in an organization. It's going to be about working in an uncluttered, easy-to-use environment.

The days of command and control are over. This is about working with the collective to tap into knowledge and skills—working iteratively inside and outside the organization.

How will companies make the move to this new environment? Not just moving, but moving quickly will be one of the biggest challenges. It's about the rate and pace of doing business. Established organizations are starting to see entrants come in who were born on the cloud—already living and breathing these technologies that are mobile and social. These new technologies bring advantages that can mean getting to market more quickly and establishing cost savings. Organizations need to move there very quickly, but they need to do it with enterprise grade. The technology has to be highly secured and trusted, and the movement has to include business processes (not just the technology).

The collaboration between employees, vendors, and suppliers will be a complete end-to-end function. There are going to be less barriers between the internal and the external because there needs to be a continuous loop and flow. We need to have the customer and value chains (partners, distributors, suppliers) in the loop to make the social aspect much more informative. It's about social in order to develop ideas and collaborate on them—to bring insights. This will be a huge boon for innovation as well as testing and getting things out more quickly, connecting the "me-to-we" across that outside chain. The future of work is really about reinventing business communications.

Bryan's Predictions on the Future of Sharing:

The future is our kids, the Millennials, who have a very different way of working than we do. They will have a big impact on business in the future.

As we evolve and change and lines continue to blur between the physical and digital world, communities will become even more important. As automation continues to replace humans for delivering information and utility, we have to ask ourselves some questions.

What will humans be responsible for? Are we headed into another renaissance of ideas, art, thinking, philosophy—the things humans have always done best? Do we trust ourselves as humans to be smarter thinkers? Technology enables us to be lazy. Will our class system continue to divide us between thinkers and non-thinkers?

The future *is* sharing, but we've become unused to it. We're always running for the goal as individuals, even as we've been trying to get our teams to collaborate more. The future will be all about opening up and sharing because the more we can get people to share, the faster we can grow as a society.

Our increased access to instant information will continue to make it faster and easier for us to solve the world's problems. When everyone can access information and share anything at any time, we truly will be a connected society. We'll be able to do anything, from mending a hole in a pair of pants to getting clean, fresh water to every human being on the planet. We'll know exactly who to go to get it done immediately, because all of the technology will be in place, and we'll be accustomed to the ease of sharing with anyone in our global tribe. Right now we're seeing threads of this fabric being woven into the human economy, but we're rapidly moving into a culture where sharing becomes whole cloth.

We need to understand and study sharing to power human business. As individuals it's up to us to have a higher consciousness about how, why, what, and where we're sharing. In the pages of this book we've laid out scenarios so you can see the impact of sharing on the things that matter to you: your family, your communities, your region, and the planet. However, it's up to us to continue to practice the study of sharing on a daily basis. Being mindful of the things you choose to share and the ripple effect it will have will naturally grow your personal brand, and the same is true for business. Stories, experiences, and ideas were all meant to be shared, so to truly bring about a sharing culture, it's every individual's responsibility to share in the very best way that we can. As I wrote in *H2H*, businesses don't have emotion, humans do, and humans are what power business.

Technology allows us all to be broadcasters, journalists, authors, inventors, and philosophers—to share ideas without limits. The future is not me sharing my ideas with you; the future is all of us channeling our inner scientists and philosophers to share with our networks, and from those networks to more networks, sharing ideas that will make a difference.

ABOUT THE AUTHOR

 Bryan Kramer is a social business strategist and CEO of the social, content, digital and demand gen agency PureMatter, located in Silicon Valley.

Bryan is the author of the bestselling book "There is No B2B or B2C: It's Human to Human: H2H" which sparked the human business movement in marketing. He consults Fortune 1000 brand executives on humanizing their business, and heads up "H2H University", an online social media training program for small to mid-size business. Bryan is a TED speaker and speaks around the world about H2H and the power of sharing.

His expertise has earned him top spots on the following noteable lists:

- The 43rd most talked about marketer by global senior marketers—Leadtail
- #26 Global Top CEO Influencer on Social Media—Kred
- Top 50 Social CEOs on Twitter Globally—Huffington Post
- Top 25 Influencer to Follow—Forbes
- The 100 Most Influential Tech People On Twitter—Business Insider Australia
- Top 9 Thought Leadership Speakers in 2015—Forbes

Bryan understands social media and how it works as a communication channel and shaper of popular culture. Quickly he has become one of the country's leading authorities on social and digital, speaking across the US and internationally on a variety of topics. As an active blogger and author, Bryan has built a community of over twenty thousand readers in his syndicated network at BryanKramer.com. He also hosts the "From the Author's Point of View" author podcast series and "The Bryan Kramer Show" as well as "#PMSubstance," PureMatter's Luminary Video Series. His #H2HChat Hangouts are Mondays at 12noon PST.

Bryan founded "H2H University" online learning courses in 2015 and personally consults Fortune 1000 executives.

Board Positions

Raynforest Advisory Board Member
HealthPure Advisory Board Member
Silicon Valley Boy Scouts Board Member

Nonprofit

No stranger to service and supporting his community, Bryan has received the highest silver medal award for community impact for his work on the executive board as VP of marketing for the Silicon Valley Boy Scouts of America. He is a past president of the American Advertising Federation (AAF)—Silicon Valley chapter and former committee member of the Boys and Girls Club of Silicon Valley and Via Rehabilitation Services. Bryan has been an active Silicon Valley Rotarian since 2006. He has been recognized by the San Jose/Silicon Valley Business Journal as a "Top Who's Who," and is a seasoned AAF National Student Advertising Competition (NSAC) judge.

Additional Agency Honors

- Webby Honoree
- "Content Marketing Campaign of the Year" from The Content Marketing Institute and Disqus
- 200+ American Advertising Federation ADDYs
- American Design Award
- Graphic Design Monthly
- PRINT Magazine International Design Annual
- W3 Interactive Awards
- Cisco Worldwide "Global Campaign of the Quarter"
- San Jose/Silicon Valley Business Journal "Fastest Growing Private Companies" and "Largest Advertising Agencies"

WEB RESOURCES

http://www.forbes.com/sites/jeffbercovici/2014/06/30/facebooks-experiment-on-emotions-sounds-creepier-than-it-was/

https://hbr.org/2014/11/from-the-knowledge-economy-to-the-human-economy (quote from Dov Seidman)

http://www.apple.com/watch

http://www.fitbit.com/

http://www.aetv.com/hoarders

http://tms.visioncritical.com/sites/default/files/pdf/sharing-new-buying-collaborative-economy-report.pdf

http://lemonly.com/work/sharing-is-the-new-buying-a-collaborative-economy-infographic

http://www.fastcodesign.com/3021522/innovation-by-design/mit-invents-a-shapeshifting-display-you-can-reach-through-and-touch

http://www.bryankramer.com/the-new-social-a-sensory-experience/

http://www.fastcompany.com/3021710/fast-feed/stumped-siri-soon-she-could-crowdsource-tough-queries

http://www.mutualmind.com/

https://us.nakedwines.com/about/index.htm

http://bryankramer.com/find-thirstier-horses-engage-employees-in-social-advocacy/

http://www.tapinfluence.com/ppc-branded-influencer-marketing-made-easy/?gclid=Cj0KEQiA9eamBRDqvIz_qPbVteABEiQAnIBTEKu77zHi7GIScAIL-uJSJMZUpWDLJv-OdQ-Tya4lehIaAhT_8P8HAQ

http://www.90daystoellen.com/

http://adage.com/section/the-viral-video-chart/674

http://wistia.com/

https://www.youtube.com/watch?v=Gw3aWPxtpfE&feature=kp_ (batkid)

https://www.facebook.com/photo.php?v=10100972302395017 (Pete Frates ALS)

http://hollywoodandvines.com/

http://www.amazon.com/Twitter-Power-3-0-Dominate-Market-ebook/dp/B00SZ633FU/ref=sr_1_1?s=books&ie=UTF8&qid=1424198345&sr=1-1

https://chrome.google.com/webstore/detail/quickpin/bhogoimaoahmedeeahleijnpljdbammj